PRAISE FOR *Turn Your Mate into Your Soulmate*

"Arielle Ford is a priestess of love, bringing forth the highest wisdom and placing it down on earth where it belongs. She has lived the love drama, learned from the love drama, and succeeded at the love drama. She has a lot of information to deliver, and in this book she does so compassionately and wisely."
—Marianne Williamson, *New York Times* bestselling author of *A Return to Love* and *A Year of Miracles*

"Arielle Ford helps us move past the unrealistic expectations and myths about love, romance, and happily ever after. In their place, she offers simple and immediate ways to breathe new life into old relationships and build bridges between the very different ways in which women and men think and see relationships."
—John Gray, *New York Times* bestselling author of *Men Are from Mars, Women Are from Venus*

"*Turn Your Mate into Your Soulmate* is a must read for all couples. This book is a profound guide toward true love, deep connection, and soul partnership. Arielle brilliantly offers a path to release all that blocks you from the soulmate love you've been longing for. I am grateful for the gifts I have received from this book."
—Gabrielle Bernstein, *New York Times* bestselling author of *Miracles Now*

"Arielle Ford guides you through a lively portal into the best relationship practices no matter where you are in your relationship journey. Reading *Turn Your Mate into Your Soulmate* is like having a super-smart big sister who absolutely has your back, giving you the lowdown on what really works. Anyone interested in deepening their relationships can benefit from this book's wisdom."

—Kathlyn and Gay Hendricks, bestselling authors of *Conscious Loving Ever After*

"Arielle Ford helps readers find their own happy ending by busting the myths spoon-fed to us by the media about love, romance, and happily ever after. Her hands-on approach to love everlasting inspires readers to create the kind of relationship with their partners that they have always wanted, desired, and so deeply deserve to have."

—Katherine Woodward Thomas, author of *Conscious Uncoupling: 5 Steps to Living Happily Even After*

"I truly believe it is important to learn from someone who has been there, done that. Arielle Ford is a perfect example of how to make a marriage not only work, but thrive. She helps you shift your perspective so you can re-create and sustain the love that once brought you together. Brilliant, practical, and transformational. Thank you, Arielle!"

—Christy Whitman, *New York Times* bestselling author of *The Art of Having It All*

"Arielle Ford reveals the secrets to creating legendary love in this beautifully written and highly prescriptive book. She offers surprisingly simple solutions for couples looking to reignite love and passion."

—Marci Shimoff, author of *Happy for No Reason*

"It's one thing to fall in love, and it's another to stay in love, survive the storms, and build a marriage that lasts a lifetime. I can *honestly* say that *Turn Your Mate into Your Soulmate* is truly outstanding—a really wonderful combination of great wisdom, useful tools, practical solutions, and heart-opening insights that can help you take your relationship from ordinary to extraordinary. Arielle Ford's book is your one-stop shop for creating the passionate, progressive, loving, and soulful partnership your heart longs for."

—Dr. Sheri Meyers, marriage and family therapist and author of *Chatting or Cheating*

"This book will show you how to transform your relationship to create more moments of deep understanding, romance, and connection . . . moments of heart opening that will create that tingly-all-over feeling."

—Sarah McLean, bestselling author of *Soul-Centered: Transform Your Life in 8 Weeks with Meditation*

"Arielle's brilliant, absolutely profound wisdom on love teaches, inspires, and proves to us all that no matter the circumstances, the most amazing love is attainable, right now."

—Kailen Rosenberg, celebrity love architect and author of *Real Love, Right Now*

"I'm in *love* with this book! A treasure trove of relationship gems that made me laugh out loud over and over. 'Pause the TV again!' I kept telling my fiancé, to read him another page. You know it's a great book when your guy is entertained, even riveted, while listening to a book over watching his beloved football!"

—Linda Sivertsen, author of *Lives Charmed* and creator of the Boyfriend Log iPhone app

"*Turn Your Mate into Your Soulmate* should be on every woman's must-read list, no matter her relationship status. This book has it all! Riveting revelations, inspiring real-life stories, woo-woo wisdom, as well as cutting-edge relationship research that *anyone* can use and implement *now* to help their relationship go from okay to good, good to great, and great to glorious. There's truly not a problem its pages can't dramatically improve or a couple it can't help reconnect—no matter how bored/resentful/annoyed they may be, for no matter how long. Arielle's decades as a 'singleton' and her ultimate incredibly happy long marriage (with its own challenges she reveals here), as well as the genius of her expert friends, infuse every page of this delightful, important read. This book is so good, I'm mad at it (while happy for Arielle and the world that she wrote it, of course!). Pick up or order twenty copies for every important woman in your life, and stand back and be amazed at what happens."

—Carol Allen, Vedic astrologer and relationship coach

"In *Turn Your Mate into Your Soulmate*, Arielle Ford masterfully guides us to reignite our soul relationship so it can shine brightly through every spring and winter of our journey together. This book will make your heart flutter all over again."

—Allison Maslan, entrepreneur and author of *Blast Off!*

"Arielle Ford has inspired legions of people to find their true soulmates. In her new book, she shares her experience and wisdom to help couples imbue their relationships with an even more soulful love and a deeper understanding of what it takes to create a true partnership."

—Rev. Laurie Sue Brockway, wedding officiant and author of *Your Perfect Wedding Vows*

"Unrealistic romantic notions of love have wreaked havoc on our relationships. Ending the myth of accidental, romantic love is our personal mission. Arielle Ford has written a book that gives couples the tools to create lasting, loving relationships instead of becoming another negative statistic about marriage failure. While men and women often differ, love is what connects them. In *Turn Your Mate into Your Soulmate*, Arielle offers crystal-clear examples and steps for you to strengthen that bridge so you can create a deep connection with your partner. This is the point of intimate relationship for your soul—your soul desires intimacy and this book shows you how."

—Orna and Matthew Walters, soulmate coaches

"I simply *love, love, love* Arielle Ford's newest book *Turn Your Mate into Your Soulmate*! Healthy and happy relationships are an integral component of inner peace, yet everyone struggles to attain the elusive ideal. Arielle keeps it real in this refreshing, honest, and inspiring book, offering the most complete and masterful guidance to truly transform marriages and encouraging us to relax into true love—and with it, true inner peace."

—Mary Allen, author of *The Power of Inner Choice*

"Arielle does it again! This time in a wonderful toolkit for seasoned couples and anyone/everyone who is interested in maintaining or bringing the magic back to their relationship. I plan on keeping the book bedside just handy to share ideas, especially the communication prompts, with my honey."

—Kim Weiss, author of *Sunrise, Sunset: 52 Weeks of Awe and Gratitude*

"Arielle Ford pulls together an amazing collection of strategies and tips not only to turn your mate into your soulmate, but to find deeper intimacy for long-lasting love."

—Cherry Norris, dating coach, actor, and filmmaker

"This is the book that every married woman should read before and during her marriage many times over. As a matter of fact, it should just stay on her bedside table."

—Christina Rasmussen, author of *Second Firsts: Live, Laugh, and Love Again*

"Arielle Ford humorously and passionately distills ageless spiritual truths in service of our greatest purpose on earth: to love and be loved. She gives us a generous and compassionate lens through which we can recognize our soul's purpose in love, and find the greatest joy in our relationships. I'm a big fan!"

—Laura Berman, LCSW, Ph.D., love and relationship expert and author of *Quantum Love*

Turn Your Mate
into Your
Soulmate

ALSO BY ARIELLE FORD

The Soulmate Secret
Wabi Sabi Love
Love on the Other Side
Hot Chocolate for the Mystical Soul (series)

Turn Your Mate into Your
Soulmate

a practical guide to
happily ever after

———— • ————

Arielle Ford

HARPERELIXIR
An Imprint of HarperCollinsPublishers

HARPERELIXIR

HarperCollins books may be purchased for educational, business, or sales promotional use. For information please e-mail the Special Markets Department at SPsales@harpercollins.com.

HarperCollins website: http://www.harpercollins.com

FIRST EDITION

Designed by Claudia Smelser

Library Of Congress Cataloging-in-Publication Data

Ford, Arielle.
  Turn your mate into your soulmate : a practical guide to happily ever after / Arielle Ford. — First edition.
    pages cm
  ISBN 978–0–06–240554–8 (hardcover)
    1. Soul mates. 2. Man-woman relationships. I. Title.
  BF1045.I58F673   2105
  306.7—dc23   2015020234

15 16 17 18 19   RRD (H)   10 9 8 7 6 5 4 3 2 1

For Claire Zammit

Thank you for sharing your ever-expanding
world of possibility, magic, and fun!

I am blessed to be showered with your love,
friendship, creativity, brilliance, and support.

Contents

This chapter clearly defines what a "soulmate" is and isn't and dispels the myths about the term to create an instant shift in perception about what's possible for your relationship. It also treats questions like "What is love?" and "Do soulmate relationships last forever?" Here we lay the groundwork for the purpose, work, and potential joy of relationship.

You'll learn how and why men are different and how to talk to them in a way that will get you what you want.

This chapter shows how letting go of your story, whether it's a victim story or your resignation that a relationship will never work, is a vital step on the path toward wholeness.

We dive deep into the nature of the soul, reincarnation as it relates to love, sacred contracts, karma, and the impact of what happens in between lives on choosing your family.

Research has shown that every couple has irreconcilable differences. This chapter recognizes ways to accept each other and thrive, in spite of the mistaken notion that we should find a way to agree on everything. You will learn to create a toolkit to help you process your emotions.

This chapter reveals the essence of finding the beauty in imperfection, or what I call Wabi Sabi Love, in your relationship.

You, your mate, and God/Spirit/Universe make up the magic triad of love. Will you love yourself and your mate unconditionally, and what does that really mean? This chapter shows you powerful steps to seek—and find—the unconditional love that will sustain your relationships in new and surprising ways.

It has been said that being in love is a socially acceptable form of insanity. This chapter provides the scientific research on the relationship between love, brain chemistry, and how to kick-start your way back to love and connection.

In basic arithmetic, one plus one equals two. In soulmate math, one plus one equals eleven, and your love blesses the world. This chapter also explains the "marriage effect" and why turning your mate into your soulmate will not only improve your own health and increase longevity and happiness, but also impact the world.

Introduction

Happily. Ever. After.

I believe these are the three most dangerous words for women in love. They imply the neatly tied-up-in-a-bow ending of a fairy-tale kingdom we were conditioned to believe exists. Real love couldn't be farther from those castles in the sky.

Even the smartest women fall into a love trance, thinking that now they have found, in their soulmate, the love of their life, that perfect elixir for all that might have gone wrong in their lives until then. During the "at-last" moment, women harbor the belief that men will naturally know how to make them happy, satisfied, and content. A love relationship with our soulmate is the perfect antidote to all that ails us. Or so we think.

We've all heard that relationships take work, commitment, and occasional sleepless nights to strike a balance. Yet so many of us believe that real "soulmate love" will somehow be different, effortless, deserved. We fully expect that our rare, precious, and unimaginable "soulmate love" will conquer everything.

And then reality settles in. Sometimes it takes a year, or ten, or twenty, but at some point we find ourselves restless—or worse: angry, frustrated, disappointed, and ready to give up. We begin to wonder whether it's time to head for divorce court. Our day-to-day reality does not match our dream of what soulmate love should reflect. Suddenly, we perceive that our Prince Charming, our once shiny knight, has turned into a rusty, stubborn barrier to happiness and fulfillment.

Even if you are blessed to be with someone who is physically, emotionally, and spiritually compatible with you, it's likely that there are days when your mate annoys you and you wish things were different.

It wasn't predictable that I would be writing a book such as this. I was a first-time bride at the age of forty-four, a late bloomer in the love department. Here's what happened. One morning I woke up very early. Before I opened my eyes, my right arm stretched across the pale-blue sheets of my queen-size bed, seeking the soft fur of my soulmate cat, J.B. J.B. wasn't in his usual spot, and as my hand searched for him I became aware of the empty, vacant space in the bed. I was suddenly hit by two dark simultaneous thoughts: "Why is my bed so empty?" and "Oh my God, I forgot to get married!"

As I was lying there, I began to replay my life in my head, trying to wrap my mind around the reality that here I was, at age forty-three, still single. It didn't make any sense to me. I knew that I was relatively attractive, fit, successful, and fun and had a great life. And yet I was alone.

The plain truth of the matter was this. I had put most of my time and energy into building my business. I was highly ambitious, and when it came to success, the more I got, the more I wanted. I had studied and mastered a variety of techniques for "manifesting" and had used them to create a career that was exceeding all of my expectations.

One of my big manifesting wins resulted in the nearly instant creation of my first business, The Ford Group, a public-relations firm based in Beverly Hills, California. I had been working for a PR firm for three years and began having thoughts about launching my own company. A part of me didn't really believe it was possible, because I had neither the money nor the specific training to open a public-relations firm on my own. However, that didn't stop me. I began to imagine what it would feel like to wake up each morning excited to walk into an office with my name on the door. I tried to envision what it would feel like to be able to call the shots about which clients I worked with and the ways I would successfully garner impressive results for them. Each day I would sit quietly and feel these feelings, using my imagination to see and feel the potential of having my own business.

After I had been doing this process for ten days, I received a phone call from a former client, Mark, who said he and his business partner wanted to take me out to lunch. I had worked with them the previous year and landed them a ton of great media spots, including an interview on *Good Morning America*. I really wasn't sure why they wanted to meet me, but I was excited to find out. After we ordered our meal, they got straight to the point.

Mark said, "We've been talking about you, and we think that it's time for you to strike out and start your own PR firm. We know how good you are, and we want to be your very first client."

Mark then reached into the inside pocket of his jacket, handed me a check in the amount of $18,000, and said, "As your first client, we are paying you our fee for one year of your services, in advance. How soon can you start?"

Three weeks later I opened The Ford Group, which quickly became a success. Clients seemed to literally fall through my door without much effort on my part. My life was busy, fulfilling, and exciting—except for my love life.

My love life up until that point had never been easy. Having grown up with two parents who didn't love—or even like—each other, I didn't have any role models when it came to love relationships. Quite simply, my love life sucked.

I began to wonder if I could apply the prayers, rituals, and processes that brought me business success in order to manifest a soulmate. I decided to find out! I made a list of all the practices I had used in the past, including creating a very specific list of my desires, prayers of gratitude for having it all easily and effortlessly delivered, daily visioning practices, and affirmations. Within a year Brian and I met at a business meeting. On the day that we met, we "knew." Everyone in the room with us "knew." Three weeks later he proposed, and a year after that we had three weddings. As a late bloomer I figured I was entitled to celebrate our union as much as possible! That was eighteen years ago.

As an older bride, I unintentionally became the poster girl for single women over forty. Often these women would pull me aside and ask, "How do I get a Brian?" I would share all the details of my process with them, and then weeks or months later they would excitedly call or e-mail me that they too now had a soulmate. Eventually my formula became the subject of my books and workshops known as The Soulmate Secret, which has now worked for tens of thousands of men and women, of all ages, in forty countries.

Once I manifested and married my soulmate, Brian, I fully expected that I had somehow skipped over the "relationships take work" part of life, because I had the perfect guy. I really believed that our relationship was special and blessed.

Like many newlyweds, I was engulfed in a delicious, super feel-good experience, my brain flooded with dopamine, oxytocin, and other wonderful neurochemicals that come with being in love. I really thought we'd be living on autopilot, happily floating through one delicious, romantic day after another.

Although I was certain that Brian was the perfect guy for me, and I believed—and still believe—we have a special relationship, I was wrong about the "skipping over" part. I came into the marriage with zero partnership skills and no working understanding of what it means to share your life with someone. I had never given it a moment's thought.

As the reality of living life with Brian set in, I quickly realized that, since I was an entrepreneur and business owner, my major strength was "being the boss." I discovered that this skill was the antithesis of what's necessary to grow and strengthen love. I hate to admit it, but I am not the most nurturing, giving person on the planet. My nature is to first think about "what's in it for me." Brian is the opposite. He is one of the most loving, generous, nurturing people I have ever met. He is a true giver. But "givers" also have needs, desires, and childhood wounds that flare up.

What I have learned is, relationships work a lot like lighting a candle. You light your partner's wick and vice versa. But sometimes the fire turns into a seemingly uncontrollable blaze. Their stuff flares up and "triggers" your stuff, and then the you-know-what hits the fan. The good news is this is normal! But in the early years of my marriage I didn't know that.

At this point in my life I had worked as a book publicist for many of the biggest names in the areas of personal growth and spirituality. I had access to countless numbers of the greatest minds who taught the secrets to being successful, happy, and fulfilled. These teachers, who were also my clients, covered a myriad of topics from meditation to manifestation—except for how to navigate love and marriage. I was 100 percent certain that Brian and I were meant to share our lives together, and I also knew that I was clueless about how to manage the moments when we were in breakdown. Prayer, meditation, chanting, vision boards, goal setting, staying positive, and saying affirmations were all part of my daily life, but none of them proved useful when my buttons were pushed to the max. During moments like these all the self-help knowledge in the world couldn't help.

Eventually, the "seeker" in me decided it was necessary to become a "student of love." I became committed to understanding the inner workings of love relationships in order to unearth the truths hidden from me for so long. From this book you will benefit from the wisdom that I discovered along my journey to create and sustain deep, fulfilling love.

Today, one of the most common questions I am asked is: "How do I *know* if he is my soulmate?" It's a great question, because there are so many myths and misconceptions about this one word. In this book you will find all of the best definitions and understandings of what a soulmate is and isn't and what it takes to grow and nurture a soulmate relationship.

In these pages you will learn how to cultivate love, minimize conflict, and create a deeper, more loving relationship. I will share the tools and skills I've learned that will allow you to see yourself and your partner in an entirely new light. They will also strengthen the bond that brought you together in the first place and ultimately take your relationship to a whole new level. Along with understanding the true nature of a soulmate comes the possibility of rediscovering the love, passion, respect, and commitment to the relationship.

This book also reveals:

- What love *really* is and what it is not

- Why we yearn to be connected to another person

- Our sacred contracts having to do with love

- Why giving up perfectionism is the key to happiness

- How to ask for and receive what you most need from your partner

- The purpose and benefits of marriage

- Components of a healthy relationship

- How to move beyond ourselves to infuse our relationship with God/Spirit/Devotion

- How to breathe new life into old love by kick-starting the fun

- Why changing partners may not be the answer and why reenvisioning the partner you have can be that path to happiness

It's one thing to fall in love and get married. It is quite another thing to have a marriage you love. Getting to that space is the true purpose of *Turn Your Mate into Your Soulmate*. It is possible. It takes initiative, commitment, and a belief that embarking on this journey to a truer relationship is worth the effort.

By the time you finish reading this book, you will know the path to get there. My dream for you is that by the final page, you will be enthusiastically in love with your beloved and living life beyond the "ever after" to the "even after."

Arielle Ford
La Jolla, California
www.arielleford.com

ONE

It's Not Supposed to Be This Way

A soulmate is someone you are attracted to
who offers you the greatest possibility for
growth for both human beings to evolve into
their greatest expression.

Debbie Ford

I t's not your fault. The magic has faded. The lights are out. You are questioning whether it is even worth fighting anymore for what you once had. The glamour is gone, and you wonder how it could possibly have slipped away. While you struggle to stay afloat in a sea of emotion, a subtle feeling of guilt mixed with despair and a dash of hope hums beneath the surface of it all.

What if I just tried a little harder? Then maybe he would change.

If you are reading this book, chances are you are indeed wondering whether you should stay or go. Should you give up on your relationship, the one you really thought was so perfect, at least in the beginning? Or is it possible to truly turn this mate, who maddens you beyond measure, into your everlasting soulmate?

It's not your fault that you are asking yourself these questions. It is merely a sign that the myth you once believed has finally been busted.

Unfortunately, you, along with most women in the modern world, have been lured into a false belief about the meaning of "true love." You were exposed to fairy-tale fantasies designed to shape you into the perfect princess waiting for her perfect prince. The media joined the conspiracy to reinforce the message of what an acceptable partner is supposed to be. You were told that, with the right clothing, perfume, house, car, children, hairstyle, career, you could turn that carefully crafted childhood fantasy into your customized reality. In essence, you were programmed to be the star in your own romantic movie with male protagonists neatly lined up to fit perfectly into the image of your hotly contended love life.

You have been brainwashed and force-fed lies.

The cartoon version of your life would go something like this. Prince Charming, outfitted in a handsome and dashing velvet suit, arrives on a white horse with the singular intention of sweeping you into his arms and onto his steed to ride off into the land of happily ever after. This awesome prince either brings you the perfect Jimmy Choo shoe or kisses you into a state of wild abandon after a long sleep.

The story promises you that Prince Charming holds the golden key to the magical land where he intuitively meets all your needs and grants your every wish. Perhaps for a brief time at the beginning of your relationship, you even experienced moments of this elusive bliss, which reinforced your belief that you had finally landed "The One."

And then life happened. Circumstances changed. Eventually, Prince Charming seemed to morph into someone you no longer recognized as your best friend, lover, and partner for life.

Let's face it. We have extremely high standards for ourselves and for our mates. Whether we know it or not, we have often turned our relationship into an unattainable goal. It is no wonder we are frustrated, disappointed, and ashamed. We often confer with our girlfriends about the annoying things our mates do, gathering stories about other horrible examples from friends of friends. This leads us down a spiral of misery, as we reinforce all that is going wrong with our relationship. We all know that what we put our attention on grows. If we are focused on venting incessantly about how bad and wrong men are, we enter the grass-is-greener-anywhere-but-here zone, distorting our vision and creating an unrealistic, perfect world we seemed doomed to never reach.

Upon further speculation, we are faced with the fact that our secret wish for a perfect life did not come true. At the same time we become stuck with these unfulfilled expectations that plague us. We try hard to put on a smile and pretend we don't feel the way we do in the hopes that no one will notice or that these intense feelings will somehow disappear if we ignore them long enough.

But we do notice them—a lot. And no amount of wishing—or venting with friends—will make them go away.

It is time for a reality check. The prince has traded in his velvet suit for a jockstrap, ripped T-shirt, or favorite pair of sweatpants. He's the guy on the couch, yelling at the game or the politician on the news, scratching his balls while he burps from his last beer. Quite honestly, was this the vision you had when you walked down that aisle, clutching a bouquet of flowers whose scent intoxicated you, and at the altar said, "I do"?

We did not realize when we uttered those words that "I do" would also mean "I do" every day.

Maybe you are familiar with the "Have you seen" syndrome? It is a phenomenon I have witnessed time and again in my own relationship and those of my girlfriends. It is as if your partner's memory gets switched off the moment you enter the room. He simply can't find anything. His wallet, shoes, briefcase, laptop, the remote, the car keys—you name it—have miraculously disappeared. It is as if his brain has been farmed out to the local post office and has temporarily gotten lost in the mail. You notice he doesn't behave that way with his guy friends. But he does with you. At first you think it is cute. Then one day you do not. And for the life of you, you cannot figure out how to re-create that initial feeling of amusement.

A variation of his sudden amnesia is expressed in another familiar syndrome I lovingly refer to as the "lost legs" syndrome. He loses his ability to walk if he knows you are there. "Honey—we got any chips?" he calls as though he himself is incapable of getting off his duff and finding them himself.

Could that really be "The One" you prayed for? "The One" God hand-selected, just for you? Is it possible you were born to be with someone who could act so common? No way! Surely you were meant for something—someone, yes anyone—greater!

Today, your relationship might be "just good enough" or "okay," but you find yourself constantly daydreaming about that elusive "real soulmate" who you know is still out there, just beyond your reach. And you might be wondering, "Do I have the courage to leave this relationship to pursue the possibility of someone new, the Right Somebody?" You know you weren't destined for mediocrity. You can feel it, and it causes you a lot of pain to see yourself living this way.

Or have things deteriorated to the point that the veil has finally been lifted to reveal your true reality? Maybe you're finally admitting to yourself that you knew as early as your wedding day you were making a mistake?

It's not your fault. None of us was ever issued the official handbook on what marriage and relationships are all about. You didn't get the memo. Most likely what you did get was the official wrapped-in-a-bow version of the "truth," the myth that says we are all destined to find our *one and only soulmate* and when we do, heavenly trumpets and harps will ring out, accompanying the rest of our days—happily ever after.

The Truth About "The One"

Let's take a second here to acknowledge that you might be royally pissed off about these circumstances. And mixed in with this anger and rage is probably a lot of sadness and disappointment. I encourage you to take a moment now, clench your beautiful hands into fighting fists, stomp your feet, and simply allow your inner princess to scream: "It wasn't supposed to be this way!"

Okay, now take a deep breath. Breathe even deeper. Now exhale. What I am about to say may not be what you expect to hear, but I am going to say it anyway.

What if it *is* supposed to be this way?

What if nature fully intended to hook us up with the one person who will hurt, offend, and annoy us the most? The person who has full access to pushing all of our buttons? What if I were to tell you the definition of "The One" includes the fact that he will be the person who will drive you to the brink of sheer madness and that his purpose in your life is to bring you to a whole new understanding of yourself?

The good news is, this same person might just be the one who is most capable of loving you most deeply and unconditionally. This person is "The One" because he gets you—both literally and metaphorically—more than anyone else.

Although all of this may seem counterintuitive, once we understand the real purpose of romantic relationships and marriage, it will make perfect sense. Before diving into that vast topic, let me share a story from an ancient time that offers one perspective on why most human beings yearn to meld their lives with another.

Many years ago, my friend Jean Houston, scholar, philosopher, and one of the foremost visionary thinkers of our time, told me a fascinating story that comes from Aristophanes, the acclaimed philosopher and comic playwright of ancient Athens. He offers a wild tale, which he shared at Plato's Symposium, about how the deep desire to spend our life with a soulmate came about.

Long, long ago in primal times there were beings who had duplicate bodies with four arms, four legs, two heads, and two sets of genitalia. They were big round roly-poly creatures that wheeled around earth like clowns doing cartwheels. They also possessed great strength. There were three types of roly-poly beings: the all-male, the all-female, and the "androgynous," who were half male and half female. The males were said to have descended from the sun, the females from the earth, and the androgynous beings from the moon.

The creatures tried to scale the heights of heaven and planned to set upon the gods. Zeus, watching them from his throne in heaven, became very jealous of all the fun the roly-polies had. He was also envious of their power. Although Zeus thought about using his thunderbolts to blast them to death, he was unwilling to deprive himself of their devotions and offerings. Instead, he decided to cripple them by chopping them in half with his sword, in effect separating the two bodies. The severed halves were then scattered in opposite directions to other parts of the world.

Aristophanes claimed that this is why we are born with the innate need to find our "other half." It's why when a half finally does meet its other half, both become deliriously happy and overjoyed with the promise of new love and delight. They believe, at least for a while, that they are complete now that they are reunited with their other half, thus obtaining "wholeness." It's as if we are genetically encoded to be mated.

What neither this story nor any of the fairy tales bothers to reveal is that this "wholeness" comes at a cost. To become whole, we must first recognize and heal our childhood wounds, all the places within us where we didn't get our needs met by our parents or principal childhood caregivers. It is our mostly unconscious wounds that, without our realizing it, create havoc and tension in our love relationships. Unfortunately, the majority of us never learned or had role models to demonstrate how to have a loving, kind, supportive, and successful relationship. We weren't given the necessary skills to navigate the inevitable conflicts that arise in relationships, leaving most of us to struggle in the deep end of emotional turmoil, acting out whatever we witnessed as children.

Most of us did not grow up with parents who modeled excellent communication skills. Perhaps your childhood environment introduced you to a dysfunctional adult relationship dynamic. Perhaps you witnessed the silent, seething passive-aggressive streak that accompanies too many family interactions. Perhaps you grew up in the fog of a hostile, verbally or physically abusive parental relationship. We absorbed these lessons and then sought out the exact person who would reinforce what we had learned. For better or for worse, there is no person better suited to kick up all your issues than your soulmate.

What a Soulmate Is . . . and Is Not

"Soulmate" is one of those heavily charged words that has a different meaning for just about everyone. Personally, I believe that a soulmate is first and foremost someone you feel physically and emotionally safe with. Someone you can completely be yourself with, someone with whom you share unconditional love, and when you look into the person's eyes, you have the experience of being "home." If you accept that definition, you will see we all have many soulmates in our lives—not just our romantic partner, but also possibly our children, parents, siblings, friends, coworkers, even our pets!

Here are several other definitions expanding on the notion of soulmates that I find extremely accurate:

A soulmate is someone who has locks that fit our keys, and keys to fit our locks. When we feel safe enough to open the locks, our truest selves step out and we can be completely and honestly who we are; we can be loved for who we are and not for who we're pretending to be. Each unveils the best part of the other. No matter what else goes wrong around us, with that one person we're safe in our own paradise. Our soulmate is someone who shares our deepest longings, our sense of direction. When we're two balloons, and together our direction is up, chances are we've found the right person.

RICHARD BACH

People think your soulmate is your perfect fit, and that's what everyone wants. But a true soulmate is a mirror, the person who shows you everything that is holding you back, the person who brings you to your own attention so you can change your life.

ELIZABETH GILBERT

A soulmate is an ongoing connection with another individual that the soul picks up again in various times and places over lifetimes. We are attracted to another person at a soul level not because that person is our unique complement, but because by being with that individual, we are somehow provided with an impetus to become whole ourselves.

EDGAR CAYCE

[With your soulmate] you open your heart knowing that there's a chance it may be broken one day, and in opening your heart you experience a love and joy that you never dreamed possible.

BOB MARLEY

One of the biggest myths about soulmates is that we each get only one big love in a lifetime. This is simply not true. The good news is that we all have many, many possible soulmates in every lifetime. I often tell my students that I believe finding the soulmate is the easy part. The hard part is learning to live with and continuously stay committed to your soulmate. It requires a daily dose of dedication, devotion, and practice. Those couples who are newly in love never quite believe me. In the "magical thinking" of rapid-fire doses of dopamine and oxytocin in the brain, it's hard to conceive of the day when your soulmate may be viewed as your highly annoying and unwanted cell mate.

It may feel as if falling in love is a trick of nature. When we meet someone we consider special, everything clicks. We are filled with deliriously happy feelings, and everything is just so "right." And then one day, boom! It feels as if a cannonball has been shot into the center of our chest and suddenly we are in the depths of misery. Our bright and shiny beloved is the source of immense pain and doubt.

> The soul is the highest, most noble part of yourself.
>
> *Gary Zukav*

It happens to virtually everyone. I was completely unprepared when this happened to me. When Brian and I met, it was simply and literally magical. We both knew on that day eighteen years ago that we were meant to spend our lives together. We got engaged and were married a year later. Like most couples newly in love, we found each other endlessly fascinating. Every time we were together, water tasted wetter, air smelled sweeter, and life was a giant bowl of cherries.

And then one day, during a completely ordinary moment of an ordinary day, just hanging out in my office, "it" happened. Suddenly my mellow and nearly always happy Brian seemed mad at me.

I heard him say, "You're not listening to me."

Immediately defensive, I shot back that indeed I was. I even recounted the exact words he had said.

But he persisted. "No, you weren't paying attention. You're *always* too busy checking your e-mail. You just don't seem interested in what I have to say."

The tension in the air was thick and uncomfortable. This was new territory. I had never heard that tone of voice before. I felt as if I were five years old and I were being accused of being "bad" or "wrong." It felt horrible.

Somehow we got past it. I apologized for appearing not to listen. He apologized. And that, I thought, was that.

Until it happened . . . again. And again. And again.

Being relatively smart, I tried to remember to stay focused and present when Brian and I were having a conversation, but it wasn't easy. I have never been a good listener. Brian wasn't the first man to point this out to me.

I am always in my head thinking, and when someone else is talking, sometimes my own thoughts seem more interesting to me and I disappear. I refer to it as my tendency to "drift" or space out.

The pattern was clear. I would drift, or Brian would perceive that I was drifting and not listening. He would then bring it to my attention, after which I would hear his words as accusatory and angry. I would get defensive and things would get icky. I don't recall how many years this pattern continued, but luckily we figured it out.

Brian was the youngest in his family. With two older brothers, a trial attorney for a father, and a feisty mother, he, as the youngest, felt he had to fight to be heard. In my family, I was the oldest of three. I was always more interested in my own thoughts than anyone else's. Somewhere in my childhood I developed a fear of making mistakes and being accused of being bad or wrong. The second I feel as if I am being accused of wrongdoing, I immediately become defensive. It turns out our childhood wounds are a perfect match to trigger each other.

Has the issue totally disappeared? No. Somehow, even with all the awareness of our individual "stuff," every once in a while, when we least expect it, there it is again.

Our occasional run-ins serve as a reminder about the things we have to learn from each other. They actually provide a certain level of constancy, however annoying they can be.

Harville Hendrix and his wife and teaching partner, Helen LaKelly Hunt, have been studying relationships for more than forty years. As therapists and researchers, they are the cocreators of Imago Relationship Therapy. It is immensely popular because of its simplicity.

Imago suggests that the purpose of partnering up is to complete our childhood and heal the wounds we experienced as a child. We seek a partner who has many of the characteristics of our parents and caregivers in the unconscious hope that they will help us to feel whole again.

Does this mean that we marry our mother or father? Pretty much. The partner we choose ends up being a mash-up of all our caregivers rolled into one. This ideal person is called our "imago," or perfect image. We unconsciously fantasize that if we can get this perfect image to love us just the way we want, then the pain we felt as a child, when we did not get our needs met, will go away and we will be healed.

Because we find partners who help us complete the unfinished business of childhood, our adult relationships and struggles feel familiar, because they remind us of our primary caretakers. These relationships present us with the opportunity to heal past wounds and find deep relational fulfillment. But it's an opportunity, not a guarantee.

The researchers believe that on an unconscious level we have a built-in "mate selector," a sort of filter, built in from childhood, that determines who we're going to select for an intimate partner in adult life. That selector is constructed out of our interactions with our parents. It is designed to filter in someone who will trigger in us the painful emotional experiences we had with our parents in childhood. These will be needs that weren't met, but often needs we are unaware of.

So we meet someone and fall in love, and it appears that the two of us are in sync about nearly everything. This is the so-called honeymoon phase, in which life is grand. Then, as if hit by lightning, we are smacked with a new sense of reality that settles deep into our bones. Suddenly, we feel compelled to say something like, "Oh my God! I am feeling just like I did when I was around my father," or, "The way you're looking at me reminds me of my mother." A sandstorm of emotions overtakes us as our old, core wounds come to the surface. It is a painful, yet necessary process to draw us closer to our partner. As paradoxical as it sounds, he is the one who will help us move beyond that pain by reminding us of its origins.

Sharing your greatest fears with another is a great act of trust and intimacy. Harville Hendrix's story is one in which his revealing his utmost fears to his wife brought them closer than ever.

For years, Harville struggled with his wife's lack of punctuality and her inability to let him know when she might be running late. He would worry endlessly until she arrived, wasting lots of energy on something he couldn't control. It had nothing to do with Helen at all. His reaction to her being late had to do with the traumatic death of his mother when he was six.

Harville's mother had gone to the pecan orchard on their small farm in southern Georgia to pick up pecans. Suddenly Harville was aware of adults rushing to the pecan orchard. In a few minutes they returned carrying his mother, who had obviously collapsed. They put her to bed and then put Harville to bed. The next morning one of his uncles gently awakened him and said, "Your mother is dead. Would you like to see her?" He then took Harville to another room where his mother was lying. In that moment Harville's mind made the connection between his mother's going off to the pecan orchard and not returning again alive.

Once Harville shared this story with Helen, she was able to identify the source of his reaction. Together they came up with a plan that she would call to let him know she was fine whenever she was going to be late. It made a world of difference on two accounts: Harville felt heard, and Helen could respond in a way that allayed his worries. By working through Harville's deep-seated issue, they both attained a new level of appreciation for one another and could see each other in an entirely new light.

Harville says that the breaking of the illusion is one of the most shocking and terrifying experiences of married life. And, just as being in love has a specific brain chemistry, this phase also has an actual change in brain chemistry—levels of dopamine fall while levels of cortisol rise—as we go from excitement to frustration, fear, conflict, and opposition. Harville writes:

> Our unconscious need is to have our feelings of aliveness and wholeness restored by someone who reminds us of our caretakers. In other words, we look for someone with the same deficits of care and attention that hurt us in the first place. So when we fall in love, when bells ring and the world seems altogether a better place, our old brain is telling us that we've found someone with whom we can finally get our needs met. Unfortunately, since we don't understand what's going on, we're shocked when the awful truth of our beloved surfaces, and our first impulse is to run screaming in the opposite direction.

Having a soulmate is a beautiful dance toward wholeness if you're willing to allow and learn from the inevitable messy bumps that go with the territory of being in a relationship. The great news is you are no longer a child. You are an adult who is fully equipped to move beyond those original wounds to a deeper center within yourself. Your soulmate is like a companion on your way to that place of healing.

Matt Licata, a psychotherapist and publishing editor from Boulder, Colorado, describes the soulmate partner as "a wild tour guide to take you into the vast, pregnant reality of wholeness." Although we often demand that our partners be able to somehow magically resolve our emotional issues and offer

> I believe that the soul is the essence of who and what we are. It comes with codes and possibilities of who we are and who we will become. It is the lure of our becoming.
>
> *Jean Houston*

what Matt calls "a final resting place where the vulnerability, burning, and tenderness" might subside, the reality is vastly different:

> Though it is not easy, you are seeing that it is through your vulnerability, sensitivity, and broken openness that love is able to make use of your body, of your psyche, of your tenderness, to emerge out of the stars and bless this weary world. Honor the fire that is raging within, for it is the link to the unfolding of pure being.

Our soulmates accompany us on our journey while we are broken wide open. In fact, it is in the very brokenness that our wholeness can emerge through the love we experience for one another. Every one of us has a distinct path that we must take. Just as no one can breathe for us, we must complete the journey ourselves.

What Is Love and How Is It Different from "Being in Love"?

Some scientists even refer to being in love as a form of addiction. When we are in love, we actually "crave" another human being and want to consume that person in every way possible. In this state we call "being in love," our brain chemistry puts us in an irresistible and heightened state of euphoria.

Through the use of CAT scans, scientists can actually look at the different parts of our brain when we are in love and observe them "light up." Being in love is a measurable event. And as we all know, the crazy roller coaster of brain chemistry it brings with it doesn't last.

Being in love is nature's way of bringing us together; staying together, however, requires more than just brain chemistry. Real love, the kind that lasts a lifetime, is the work of emotionally mature adults who put aside the fairy tales of "happily ever after" in exchange for, as my good friend Katherine Woodward Thomas says, happily *even* after.

The two most important things to understand about love can be summed up in this way: love is both a choice and a behavior. Every day we choose whom we love and we choose to express this love through loving behaviors. The term "unconditional love" means that although we may not always "like" what our partners are doing, we choose to love them—all of them—the good, the bad, and the ugly. This doesn't mean we will put ourselves at risk; we may have to love those people from afar if they become a danger to us.

This book is *not* about vitriolic relationships. It is *not* about how to manage relationships turned toxic, harmful, or abusive. If you are in an extremely negative relationship in which you see no way out, seek counseling. That may be the right avenue to help you move forward. If you are in a state of disappointment, frustration, or anger, keep reading, because this book is about getting you back on the path to finding the deepest love possible with your partner of choice.

In order to navigate your relationship successfully, it helps to understand what love is—and what it is not. Love is not possessive. A violent bout of jealous behavior does not mean someone loves you. It means the person feels threatened, which often turns into threats directed at the closest person—*you*. Love is not about blaming other people, making them wrong for who they are or attempting to control them by spying on them, secretly checking their smartphones for messages, or other distrustful behaviors. Love is not about any of those things.

Love is connection. Love is a feeling. Love is the juiciest part of life. Love opens our heart, expands our world, and brings a smile to our lips. For love we make commitments and agreements to share our life with another in good times and in bad.

When we pledge our love to another we say: "I will love you on your good days and your bad days. I will be your safe place to land. I will share with you my attention, affection, and appreciation. With you I will become a better woman and with me you will become a better man. I will be your best friend, lover, partner, and protector. If things don't work out, I won't sell you out."

Love is not all things shiny and sparkling. Although they are nice for a special day, they are not ultimately what love is all about. Love is as much about giving as it is about receiving. And it's also about being willing to forgive. And let's not forget that love is also about truth telling.

Love is God. Love is *who* we are. Love is why we are here.

To put it simply, love is all there is. Everything else is an absence of the very purpose for being on this earth. That is the reason it is confusing, hurtful, and disheartening when our expectations of how love should show up in our lives are not met.

Would you believe me if I told you the ingredients to your reawakened love are within your reach after all? That your situation is not a lost cause? That however things turn out between you and your partner, you are on the right path after all? How do I know this? Because if you were not, you would have stopped reading by now. That means you hold hope in your heart for a new way of being, and that is the first step to healing.

You may not believe me just yet, but it is possible to rediscover that attractive, funny, attentive mate you once knew. Your now boring life can be transformed as you recapture that magic you once had, obtaining a level of closeness and connection in your relationship unlike anything you've ever had.

You didn't know you had these amazing, transformative powers, did you? Well, you do. Everyone does. It doesn't take "work," it's not "hard," and it doesn't require years of expensive therapy or tons of time. In fact, you don't even have to have "the talk" with your partner to experience the change you seek.

You will need a few tools to accompany you on this journey of transformation. You'll need the desire to improve your relationship, the willingness to try new things, and the right strategy. It will require a few tweaks, but nothing major. And because I never talk about anything I haven't tried myself, I promise you these minor shifts won't hurt a bit. In fact, they will feel so good, you'll be begging for more.

Are you ready to have more love and less fear? More laughter and less rage? More energy and less stress?

Stay with me now. I've only just gotten started.

TWO

Understanding Men

The Martian, the Hero, and the Cave Dweller

I am weird, you are weird. Everyone in this
world is weird. One day, two people come
together in mutual weirdness and fall in love.

Dr. Seuss

The sky was streaked with a magnificent array of pink and amber light against the light gray clouds of a late November afternoon. We were sitting on the bank of the Ganges in Rishikesh, India, with a dozen of our friends, watching a holy man with a big head of hair, a long beard, and simple orange robes officiate at a Hindu wedding.

The bride was resplendent in her scarlet sari, adorned with ropes of gold jewelry from her forehead to her jingling ankles. The groom wore a turban on his head and a traditional Indian silk suit. They both looked regal and yet very solemn. Unlike at American weddings, no one seemed to be smiling.

At the end of the ceremony, the holy man and the wedding couple walked from a platform onto the stone ledges not far from us and sat amid eighty young boys, all wearing yellow robes. It was now time for the daily sunset *aarti*, a sacred ceremony that includes the lighting of candles, chanting, and offerings. We had paid a small number of rupees to buy the offerings, which consisted of little palm-frond nests filled with flower petals and a small candle to infuse our prayers into before we set them free upon the rapid current of Mother Ganga.

The holy man and several women wearing orange saris led the choir of boys and everyone around them in a series of chants. Every once in a while he would stop and converse with the wedding couple. Although we couldn't understand what he was saying, several times we heard him say in English, "Okay, honey," and the couple and everyone else would burst out laughing. Finally we got to see a few smiles from the bride and groom.

At the end of the ceremony, we wandered over to the twelve-foot wrought-iron arch marking the entrance to an ashram. It was here that our little group had agreed to congregate before heading back to our motel in the nearby holy city of Haridwar. While waiting for our group to assemble, I noticed a Western woman in orange robes walking past me at a very fast pace. I instantly recognized her from an HBO special on India we had watched many times, and I called out to her.

With a big smile, she turned around and said to me, "Would you like to meet Swamiji?"

Of course I agreed and then explained I had nearly a dozen friends with me, to which she replied, "No problem. Bring them too!"

Within minutes we were all sitting at the feet of the guru and a lovely American woman, second in command at the ashram, Sadhvi Bhagawati Saraswati. The guru of the Parmarth Niketan ashram, Pujya Swamiji, spoke perfect English and encouraged us to ask him or Sadhvi anything we wanted to know.

Not being shy, I quickly raised my hand and asked, "What were you saying to the wedding couple that ended with 'Okay, honey'?"

Swamiji laughed and explained. "I told the groom that the key to a successful marriage is very simple. Anytime his wife asks him for something, his automatic response should always be 'Okay, honey.'"

The guru wasn't proposing that the groom be in false agreement with his bride, but rather that he offer respectful consent to his wife's needs. He gave the couple two words that convey understanding, listening, and respect, two words that can make all the difference.

Harmony, or at least the absence of all-out war, is what most people desire in a long-lasting relationship. I am pretty certain your spouse didn't wake up this morning wondering how he could drive you crazy today.

In fact, there's a very good chance that he would love to know *exactly* what would need to happen in order to make your day one of the best ever. Nothing would make him happier than to see you happy.

You don't believe me, do you? You're probably thinking, "Oh, he knows precisely what I want from him. I tell him every day, all day long. If only he would remember to pick up his wet towels off the bathroom floor, and put the cap back on the toothpaste, and take the garbage out, and help Johnny with his math homework . . ."

Sound familiar? Just as we didn't get the owner's manual on how to live happily ever after, the powers that be also forgot to give us the instructions for understanding men. Most women live as if men are simply what my friend and relationship expert Alison Armstrong calls "hairy versions of ourselves." We expect men to think like us, react and respond like us, and behave a certain way. And when they don't, we are surprised, disappointed, and frustrated.

My girlfriend's sister, Leslie, constantly complains that her husband leaves his dirty socks everywhere. She has even started naming them as she wanders around the house, picking up after him with a scowl on her face. She wonders why he can't seem to hear her every time she yells at him about his messiness. The angrier she gets, the more reticent he becomes.

The good news is the cycle of misunderstanding can be broken, once you discover some simple issues that separate men from women. When you recognize these areas, it will give you the key to easily getting what you want from your partner. It is not about manipulating him, but understanding where he is coming from to increase the chances of both parties getting their needs fully met.

Male culture is not the same as female culture. As Dr. John Gray explained more than twenty-five years ago in his international bestseller *Men Are from Mars, Women Are from Venus* (a classic that still resonates today, even though it was one of the first books to examine the different mind-sets of men and women), men aren't women and women aren't men. Once we understand the differences between the two genders, we can solve a multitude of relationship issues.

Let me be clear. We lead busy lives, and I would be the last person to add yet another thing to your to-do list. I am not talking about doing more; I am actually talking about doing less—and about doing it in a different way. Think of it as applying your best intercultural skills to every interaction with your partner.

John Gray suggests that men need to feel as though their women view them as a hero. It's genetic. It is a part of who they are. "Basically," Gray says, "men are not motivated if there is no reward."

Truth be told, who is? We all like to be rewarded for the good work we do. Women tend to find reward through connection, while men tend to find reward through action. That difference alone can create a lot of trouble, if we overlook how each experiences the reward he or she seeks. Gray suggests that men and women are motivated by very different things. "Men are motivated when they feel needed, while women are motivated when they feel cherished." Can you relate?

Have you ever asked yourself, "Why do I need a man?" According to Gray, women need men so they don't have to do it all alone. Women need men in order to feel that there is someone who will support them in being whoever they want to be. It is not about *codependency*; it's about *interdependency*.

Men are drawn and attracted to women who give them the sense that the women feel really lucky to be with them, like they really scored to be with such a terrific guy. Gray claims the man wants to feel that you're the luckiest woman in the world, because he has something that can make you really happy. He wants to be the key that fits your lock or—to borrow a fairy-tale phrase—the shoe bearer who has the right size, just for you.

When a man can provide for you, whether it is emotional support, taking out the trash, painting the house, or cooking a good meal, telling him how good it makes you feel to have that kind of support, how happy it makes you, makes him overjoyed.

Man Talk

According to a team of researchers at the University of Pennsylvania, women's brains are literally wired differently from men's. While the female cortex has a stronger tendency to be connected between the right and left hemispheres, an arrangement that fosters emotional processing and intuition, the male cortex is found to be more connected to rear brain areas, such as the cerebellum, which allows for greater coordination between perception and action.[1] If we know our differences in thinking stem from our physiology, we can find a way through simple techniques to understand one another.

Now take another deep breath, because what I am about to say may seem as if you're going to have to take it all on yourself. You don't. Understanding how men think will make it a lot easier to relate to them. Because we know women tend to be stronger in making emotional connections, we can leverage that skill to our advantage. That's the point of the following exercise.

When you ask him a question, for instance, follow relationship expert Alison Armstrong's advice. She suggests putting a piece of imaginary masking tape over your mouth. Give him as much time as he needs to answer. Men prefer to do one thing at a time. If you ask him two questions in a row, you will confuse him. My girlfriend once asked her husband to roll down the window and take an exit at the same time. They almost drove off the road.

When your partner answers you, don't respond with another question. He literally needs a sentence that shows you are listening before moving on to the next thing. According to John Gray, repeat a phrase such as, "Well, that makes sense," or "That's a good idea," or "Tell me more about that." And then share your opinion about what he said. John Gray says men bond with you when they feel you are listening to them.

Gray also says your tone of voice is a critical component of good communication. If there is an emotional tone to your voice that is frustrated or hurt, rather than happy and delighted, a man tends to grossly exaggerate the meaning of your tone. Suddenly, through his own misinterpretation, he will feel he is no longer in hero mode. Fallen heroes make for terrible listeners, lovers, and friends.

That doesn't mean you should pretend everything is all right, that you shouldn't share your feelings. Sharing emotions is critical to the health of any relationship. It simply requires the proper setup to prevent misunderstandings. During the times you need to say things just to share your feelings, start with a simple prelude such as, "Honey, I just need to talk about my feelings for a few minutes, and then I'm going to feel so much better. I just need you to listen. You don't have to fix anything; you certainly don't have to change anything about you. I just want to use you as a sounding board and share my feelings." Then limit yourself to ten minutes and end with, "Thanks for letting me get that out. I feel so much better." By taking this approach, he learns that you can be emotionally upset about things, but then quickly recover.

Tapping into Your Partner's Inner Hero

Remember my girlfriend's sister, Leslie? The one who was trapped in an endless cycle of complaining about messiness and being met each time with resistance from her spouse? You may find yourself in a similar position, having asked your partner to take out the trash or pick up his dirty clothes. Perhaps you have used the most delightful tone of voice over the years, or maybe you have screamed it a million times in a glaring, shrill way. Either way, nothing worked, right?

Our frustration stems from yet another myth we have been spoon-fed: "If he really loved me, he would know what I want and need from him." Or how about this one? "If he would just pay attention, and if he really wanted to make me happy, it's obvious what needs to be done."

Only it isn't obvious. It's like a Dutch person speaking to a German. The sounds seem similar, but oftentimes the words have a different meaning.

Men don't hear what we say in the way we assume they should. We think we are speaking their language, but we are not. We are saying "mauve," and they hear "pink."

To avoid misunderstandings, a slight shift in formulation can make a huge difference. Let's pretend you are hungry. You say to your partner: "Hey, would you like to go out to dinner tonight?" He, however, is not hearing that you are asking to eat at a restaurant. What he is hearing is that you don't want to cook for him. Although you are pretty sure that you have just let him know what you would like, his thoughts are elsewhere. He hears the words, but infers a completely different meaning. Why does this happen?

It comes down to what motivates men versus what motivates women. First and foremost, men want their thoughts to be respected, just like us women, but it is equally important to them to know what their actions provide for us.

In her bestselling book *The Queen's Code,* Armstrong explains it this way: "To a man nothing is worth doing, but much is worth providing." By this Armstrong means that asking a man to do a particular chore without telling him what this action "provides" for you does not give him a way to win. Men are all about winning points and not much about doing something just for the sake of doing it. Men need to really get the "benefit" of what they are providing for you. "Providing" gives them purpose. Men naturally want to provide for women, but so many women are used to providing for themselves these days. The result is a form of emasculation for them. Then they shut down because they figure they have nothing to contribute. Their thought is then, "Why do it, if my wife can do it instead? She doesn't need me." Thus, the cycle of misunderstanding continues.

In an interview with Alison, she provided me with another helpful example of how to avoid this type of misunderstanding. Let's suppose you say to your guy, "Honey, let's go to a movie tonight!" and he responds by simply saying no. You might be hurt by his response and feel rejected.

But here's the deal. The reason he declines isn't what you think. In his mind, he's thinking, "It's Friday night. I'm tired. I just want to relax."

Although it is the truth and might even help you understand what he is really thinking, he won't share it with you because, according to Alison, it is not natural for men to provide a counteroffer. So you end up feeling as though he doesn't want to spend time with you. Only that isn't the case at all. It is all about the language you use that will give you the result you are looking for.

A more powerful approach looks like this: "Honey, I would really like to spend some time with you and connect with you, so could we go to a movie this weekend?" Results-oriented language gives your partner the information he is looking for. He needs to know the effect his action would have on you. When it is formulated in this way, he isn't limited to "tonight"; he has options and he understands what you are really asking for is togetherness time.

Marital expert Dr. Patricia Allen claims that a man's deepest desire is to have his thoughts respected. Relationship coach Mat Boggs takes the idea even farther, saying that most men would rather have respect than sex! He states, "We have a deepseated desire to provide and deliver happiness to women."

So it is not that our partners don't want our happiness. It is quite the opposite! When we learn to speak in a way in which they can hear us, they will indeed do what we need to be happier.

Let's look at a few examples:

1. You want him to take out the trash. Next time try this: "Honey, when you take out the trash for me, I feel like a treasured queen who is adored and loved by her king

who saves her from dealing with those heavy, stinky cans."

2. You want him to close the garage door: "Honey, when the garage door is closed, I feel safe and protected in our home, and feeling safe and protected makes me happy."

3. You want him to make dinner reservations without asking you where you want to go: "Honey, after working all day and making a zillion decisions, I feel loved and ladylike when you make the decision about where we are going to dinner. It feels like the early days of when we first got together, and you created special date nights for us." Another winning approach to making this request is to formulate it in this way: "I'd love to go out to dinner with you tonight. Here are three options for restaurants that I'd like to go to. Would you decide and then surprise me?"

Another example would be something most women have had to deal with: putting the toilet seat down. All the asking, cajoling, and demanding never seems to get it done. The same goes for making the bed. Whether it's putting the toilet seat down or making the bed, we women don't get the results we want.

Armstrong says the first thing you have to give up about the toilet issue is "the expectation that 'down' is right and 'up' is wrong." Having the toilet seat up is efficient for him. An unmade bed is efficient for him. And men are all about being efficient. Although your being upset and mad at him for not doing these things may irritate him, it won't scare him, and he isn't going to do them just to keep you from being upset. What he needs is a *good* reason for putting down the toilet seat or making the bed. To do this you have to explain to him how these actions will provide something for you.

Here's how Alison solved the toilet-seat problem with her husband, Greg. She began by asking him, "Would this be a good time to tell you about something I really need?" Then she explained to him three things:

1. "To me the toilet seat is really gross. To put the toilet seat down, I have to touch it, and it becomes a yucky, 'ewww' experience!"

2. "I often have to pee in the middle of the night. When the toilet seat is up, I end up falling into the toilet, with my butt in the cold water, which is awful."

3. When he responded, "Why don't you turn on the light?" she explained, "By turning on the light I turn on my brain, and then I can't go back to sleep."

She also shared with him that by putting down the seat, he would be her hero and protect her from all these bad experiences. Immediately Greg complied. Alison noticed and began to express her appreciation the next several times she saw the toilet seat down. Problem solved!

What happens when you don't ask for what you want or need? What happens when you suppress your internal seething rage? Alison says:

> There is a huge myth in which women project onto men that they are like us and that they do things (and not do things) for the same reasons as us. Instinctively women survive by being "more pleasing and less dis-pleasing." A woman's brain has databases that track what other people prefer. We notice how they take their coffee, we notice that they always use pepper on their food, or that they like certain kinds of jokes. When we hear a man speak and he says "and then I couldn't find my socks," we make a list in our head to buy him more socks. Women are always looking for ways to please him. We think we gather this information because we love them, but actually it's a very primitive instinct.

When a man doesn't know what we need, we wrongly assume that he doesn't care enough about us. Even though you've dropped huge hints about what you would like, he doesn't hear them, because his brain doesn't work that way. Hints and subtlety are not your friends. What does work is being specific about what you want and adding in what having that provides for you.

When we don't do this, it builds resentment in both partners. He wants to make you happy. By not telling him what will make you happy, he doesn't know how to make you happy. It crushes his confidence that he will ever be able to make you happy. As a result, he enters avoidance mode, spending less time and money to make you happy, because you haven't given him information he can digest. In fact, he may start avoiding you too.

If he tries to figure it out and then fails, the downward spiral continues because you are not happy; at the same time he sees his attempts now as a bad investment of his time and energy. If he feels he can't ever make you happy, the ultimate death happens in his brain. He shifts to "I can never win" and he tries to avoid upsetting you to lessen the experience of "losing." That is when men begin to lie—so they won't upset you.

It may sound crazy, but this type of pattern is more common than you think. The way to end it is to ask for what you need in a way in which your partner can actually hear.

Asking for what you need may not come naturally to you, so it is helpful to be prepared well ahead of time. The next opportunity you have to ask your partner for something, Alison Armstrong suggests that you first *ask yourself* these questions:

- How will this make me feel?

- What will I be able to be or want to be?

- What will I be able to do or be willing to do?

- How will this change my life?

- How will this change my experience of this situation?

And then, after your honey does what you have asked, be sure to clearly and verbally articulate your appreciation for what he has provided. You may have been living as if he should already "know" that taking out the trash will make you happy, but that's not how it works. *You need to clearly articulate what your request provides.* This new way of communicating will take some practice, and Alison recommends that you practice this with all the men in your life, not just your spouse.

Men clearly have different expectations and needs than women. Sometimes the fulfillment of their needs feels in direct opposition to ours. That can be scary and threatening, but once we realize the origin of their behavior, we can put it into the proper perspective.

What Men Want More Than Sex

Are you shocked by the idea that men could possibly want something even more than sex? It's true. The idea made me confront my own stereotypes and beliefs fed by media messages such as "sex sells" and "men want it more than anything else on this earth."

It's simply not true. The first time I heard this from my friend and relationship expert Mat Boggs, I nearly fell out of my chair. I couldn't believe my ears when he told me the thing men want more than anything else is *respect.*

Research has shown that men would rather have their wives love them less than disrespect them. Shaunti Feldhahn, a nationally syndicated newspaper columnist, author, and speaker, wrote a fantastic book entitled *For Women Only: What You Need to Know About the Inner Lives of Men*. After interviewing over one thousand men, she recounts the surprising truth she learned about them. Feldhahn found that men want and need to be respected both privately and publicly.

But what does respect look like for a man? One basic definition of respect is "a deep admiration for someone you hold in high regard and treat well."

John Gray also points out that men feel respected when they can be your hero. He says that when a woman expresses her appreciation for her man, it causes the man to bond with her. He also claims that holding someone in esteem and validating them not only shows respect, but also honors them and makes them feel safe with you. Gray says, "One of the simplest ways to show your man respect is this: We love to have our thoughts respected and honored. Anytime you say to us, 'That's a great idea' or 'What you just said is brilliant,' we just light up!"

Simply put, your man wants to hear about all the things he is doing "right" and all the ways he is making you happy. He feels very respected when you acknowledge him in front of friends and family, and you get extra bonus points too.

Boggs offers the top four forms of respect:

> In any relationship that works, there is I, You, and We. In a connected relationship, the objective is to continue to grow both personally and as a couple. You shouldn't have to give up who you are or who you want to be for the sake of the relationship.
>
> *Otto Collins*

1. Keep agreements—do what you promise to do.

2. Listen to and acknowledge his communications.

3. If you must offer constructive feedback, always do it in private.

4. Celebrate him in public.

In looking at this list of ways to respect your partner, it is clear they want what we want. We want our partners to do what they say they will do, listen to us, offer helpful feedback that doesn't smack of hateful criticism, and celebrate and acknowledge us in front of others.

If we want the same things, why do we often have such a hard time seeing it in the other person? It is not the substance that differs, but the form it takes. The real difference is the delivery, not the intention behind it.

Cave Time

Have you ever noticed that your guy sometimes decides to "disappear" physically or emotionally after a particularly lovely night or weekend together? Or he just occasionally detaches, although there doesn't seem to be any rhyme or reason for it?

This is perfectly normal, a type of behavior often referred to as "cave time." It is a moment in time when a man needs to disconnect and restore himself. This concept isn't new. Dr. John Gray introduced it over twenty years ago in his *Men Are from Mars, Women Are from Venus*. Gray likens a man's intimacy cycle to a rubber band: "When they pull away, they can stretch only so far before they come springing back," he told me in an interview once. "This cycle involves getting close, pulling away, and then getting close again. Most women are surprised to realize that even when a man loves a woman, periodically he needs to pull away before he can get closer."

Gray notes that women misinterpret a man's pulling away, because women generally pull away for different reasons, such as when they are hurt, don't trust men to understand their feelings, or have been disappointed. Men are pulling away only to fulfill their need for independence and autonomy, says Gray, but once they get a little time alone, they will come back ready to love again.

Dating coach Carlos Cavallo explains it this way:

Men usually disconnect or unplug from a relationship to recapture their sense of masculinity. Most of the time it has nothing to do with their woman. He just doesn't completely feel like a man when he's intensely connected to a woman for too long a period. He needs to connect in cycles. It's a lot like catching your breath after exercising. The exercise feels fantastic, but you need to catch your breath and then come back with renewed focus and energy.

Cavallo calls this a "disconnection feedback loop."

Unfortunately most men don't even try to explain this to their partners or aren't even aware of it themselves. Many women end up feeling their men pulling away, and their emotional alarms go off. Some even experience downright panic.

The solution is quite simple. First, realize that this is normal and have a game plan for yourself. Don't try to talk him out of it, don't ask him how long he will be in his cave, but rather use it as an opportunity for your own me-time or time with girlfriends. If you are worried about your partner's need for time with the guys, for instance, remember what John Gray says. Although we may not always like to admit it, men need cave time and women crave time with their girlfriends too.

Love Requires Trust

Allowing for time away from each other requires a certain level of trust, a key component that can either add to or detract from the health of your relationship. Have you ever asked yourself how much trust you have in your partner? The truth is, trust really starts with trusting yourself, much like love: you cannot love another fully until you can show that same love to yourself.

If you are wondering where you stand in your relationship, consider the following Trust Scale, developed by University of Waterloo professor J. K. Rempel and his team. Originally published in the *Journal of Personality and Social Psychology,* this quiz measures the level of trust in close relationships.[2] Below is an adapted version of the quiz to help you determine your trust levels. It is merely to raise your level of thinking about where some of your issues may lie in your relationship.

THE TRUST SCALE

Instructions: Using the 7-point scale shown below, indicate the extent to which you agree or disagree with the following statements as they relate to someone with whom you have a close interpersonal relationship. Place your rating in the box to the right of the statement.

STRONGLY DISAGREE			NEUTRAL			STRONGLY AGREE
-3	-2	-1	0	1	2	3

1. My partner has proven to be trustworthy, and I am willing to let him/her engage in activities that other partners find too threatening.

2. Even when I don't know how my partner will react, I feel comfortable telling him/her anything about myself, even those things of which I am ashamed.

3. Though times may change and the future is uncertain, I know my partner will always be ready and willing to offer me strength and support. ☐

4. I am never certain that my partner won't do something that I dislike or will embarrass me. ☐

5. My partner is very unpredictable. I never know how he/she is going to act from one day to the next. ☐

6. I feel very uncomfortable when my partner has to make decisions that will affect me personally. ☐

7. I have found that my partner is unusually dependable, especially when it comes to things that are important to me. ☐

8. My partner behaves in a very consistent manner. ☐

9. I can rely on my partner to react in a positive way when I expose my weaknesses to him/her. ☐

10. When I share my problems with my partner, I know he/she will respond in a loving way even before I say anything. ☐

11. I am certain that my partner would not cheat on me, even if the opportunity arose and there was no chance that he/she would get caught. ☐

12. I sometimes avoid my partner because he/she is unpredictable, and I fear saying or doing something which might create conflict. ☐

13. I can rely on my partner to keep the promises he/she makes to me. ☐

14. When I am with my partner, I feel secure in facing unknown new situations. ☐

15. Even when my partner makes excuses that sound rather unlikely, I am confident that he/she is telling the truth. ☐

Scoring: Add the numbers together and then divide by 15 to get your final score. A negative number indicates serious trust issues, while a positive number shows you exhibit greater levels of trust. The higher the number, the better.

My dear friend Vivian Glyck has been married for fourteen years. She and her husband, Mike, have an amazing twelve-year-old son, Zak, for whom they have graciously allowed us to be godparents. As in all marriages, she and Mike have experienced the full range of ups and downs, including business uncertainties, Mike's very scary struggle with stage-three cancer a few years ago, and his passage from illness to wellness again.

Curious about the effect this quiz could have on a couple such as Vivian and her husband, I asked her to take it. She found that completing the quiz gave her surprising insights into trust issues in her relationship that she didn't even know were there.

"I'm normally a fairly trusting person," she told me, "but I saw that over the years unresolved issues in our relationship, including lack of integrity about commitments made, schedule changes, or times when my husband embarrassed me in public, had made me cynical and less trusting."

She took a simple approach to eliminating these issues. "By illuminating these seemingly small, but corrosive weak spots, I was able to be more honest with myself and my partner, and we have come to agree on what is important for us to feel both safer and more trusting with each other," she concluded.

Whatever your current trust level is, it is supported by the stories you tell yourself about who you believe your partner to be. Now that we have established the different ways in which men and women interpret relationships, let's move on to the stories behind them.

Transforming Your Story

Love is composed of a single soul
inhabiting two bodies.

Aristotle

I n her book *The Proper Care and Feeding of Husbands*, Dr. Laura Schlessinger recounts a story one of her listeners found on the Internet entitled "Shopping for the Perfect Husband." The tale is set in the "Perfect Husband Land" store, a five-story building where women can go to find their perfect match. On each of the five floors there are men with various qualities. The main rule is that once you reach any given floor, you have to select a man from that floor. If you don't, you can go to the next floor, not knowing for sure what you will find. The trick was that you can't return to a lower floor unless you plan to leave the store husbandless.

Marianne and Joan, lifelong best friends, set off to find Mr. Soulmate in the enormous department store. On the first floor there was a small sign that read:

THESE GUYS LOVE CHILDREN AND HAVE GOOD JOBS.

Joan thought that was great, but she was also curious to see what was on the second floor. Marianne followed her up the escalator to the second floor, where they found a somewhat larger sign that said:

THESE GUYS ARE SUPER HANDSOME,
LOVE CHILDREN, AND HAVE GREAT JOBS.

Marianne exclaimed with delight: "Wow! Exactly what I need. Let's take a look around."

But Joan said, "No, let's go up another level and see what's there."

Marianne followed Joan with slight reluctance. But they were best friends, after all. She must be right.

On the third floor, the two women were astonished to find yet another larger sign. This time it read:

THESE GUYS ARE NOT ONLY SUPER HANDSOME,
LOVE CHILDREN, AND HAVE GREAT JOBS, BUT
THEY ARE ALSO HAPPY TO HELP WITH HOUSEWORK!

Marianne's jaw dropped. Her excitement level grew, but she could see that Joan was even more curious to see what was next. She agreed that they would see what else they could get in a husband by going up yet another floor.

The fourth-floor sign, slightly larger than the rest they had seen, virtually screamed out at them:

OUR FOURTH-FLOOR HUSBANDS ARE SUPER HANDSOME, LOVE CHILDREN, HAVE GREAT JOBS, ENJOY HELPING WITH HOUSEWORK, AND ARE GREAT IN BED!

They were on a roll now. Nothing could stop them. Convinced that the fifth floor would offer even better husband options, Marianne and Joan confidently took the escalator to the final floor. There they found a tiny torn sign that read:

THIS FLOOR OFFERS PROOF THAT WOMEN ARE IMPOSSIBLE TO PLEASE.

You may not see yourself in this story, and perhaps you are satisfied with most things in your mate. But my guess is you may have had a moment or ten in your life in which you wanted way more than your mate could offer. You left the room feeling empty-handed and somehow ripped off. Life wasn't supposed to be this way.

Oftentimes women create unreasonable expectations when it comes to their relationships. Rather than honor and celebrate the person they have, they become heat-seeking missiles of criticism and blame. In their imaginary perfect world, they fully anticipated having the perfect husband. "Perfect Husband" is the story they created. "Perfect Husband" is not real. "Perfect Husband" is the idol they created in their own imaginations. When people follow this pattern of thinking, the end result is inevitable. Anger, disappointment, and resentment arise when the story, in their opinion, is unfulfilled.

> The soul is the truth of who we are. The light, the love that is within us. Michelangelo said that when he got a big piece of marble, the statue was already in it. His job was just to eliminate the excess of all that was not the statue. Our job is to get rid of the excess, useless fear that hides the light of our soul.
>
> *Marianne Williamson*

This is what we human beings do. We make up stories about how things should be. But what if we were to change the plot completely? As directors in our own life movie, we have the option. The question is whether we have the courage to take that leap of faith.

One of my all-time favorite sayings is that we live in a "both/and world." It's *both* the way you say it is *and* the way I say it is.

Our perception of life and the world is very personal. It is shaped by our interpretation of what has happened. Two people can witness an accident and come away with very different explanations of what they saw. Both believe they are speaking the "truth," because for them it is *their* truth. And yet we know that every story has two or more sides.

As we grow up, we constantly try to make sense of the world around us. During our maturing process, we do the best we can with our young, unformed minds. Quite often we misinterpret what is actually happening and end up concluding that something bad is happening. Even worse, we often think it's our fault.

What is your defining story? We all have a few. I bet you can even pinpoint the moment that you experienced something that created the belief system about yourself that you have carried with you all your life. For me it was one moment in time that I will never forget.

The one event that shaped the first forty years of my life occurred when I was three or four years old. I was attending a service at a temple with my family. The president of the temple, Sy Mann, was sitting in front of us. Several people in the congregation were talking to each other while the rabbi was speaking. I heard him say to the person next to him that he wished everyone would shut up.

I don't know what compelled me to do this, but I began walking up and down the aisles in my pretty pink dress and black patent-leather shoes, shouting at the top of my little-girl voice: "Sy Mann says to shut up!"

And with that, several hundred people turned around and laughed at me. I was ashamed, devastated, embarrassed, humiliated, and confused. My immediate critical decision was to never, ever bring attention to myself again. And for sure I would not be speaking to a large crowd. Ever.

Fast-forward to college. I signed up for Public Speaking 101. Of course, standing up in front of the class to speak was a big part of the curriculum. On my very first attempt at public speaking, I walked to the podium and promptly passed out.

On my second try, I walked to the podium and passed out before I could say five words.

On my third trip to the front of the room, I again collapsed onto the floor. Then the professor tossed me out of the class. He just couldn't take it anymore. Neither could I.

My childhood belief that speaking out loud to a group of people would result in being embarrassed and humiliated had become "my story." As with any story based on past hurts that we tell ourselves, mine had a long-term negative effect on my life.

Many years later at a workshop we did a process to unconceal the "story" that shaped our life, and this ancient memory of the temple incident came bubbling up. I saw that this "story" was holding me back from my greatest potential on many levels. Not only was I unable to do any public speaking; I often went out of my way to not be noticed, to stay in the background and out of the limelight. As a publicist, my career was all about being "behind the scenes." It was my job to make people visible and potentially famous. I remember telling friends and clients that I didn't want to be famous, but I did want to be able to "whisper into the ears of power."

I had spent decades stuck in my story, that I was meant to live a life "behind the scenes." This story limited my potential and shut down all possibility of sharing all of my gifts. On a certain level, I was a victim of my story.

During this workshop I had the opportunity to examine this story and rewrite it. As an adult I could now see that all the people who laughed at me that day were simply enjoying the audacity of a little girl trying to do something good. I made up a new story: on that day in temple I was so cute and adorable that the adults were smiling and laughing as a way to positively acknowledge me. Which story is true? Both!

My life changed the day I changed my story. I wasn't an overnight success, and I did not instantly become a stellar public speaker. At the same time, I was finally willing to begin the process of learning how to get comfortable in front of a crowd. It was a timely and useful exercise, because soon after I embraced my new story, my first book came out from one of the world's top publishers. A fifteen-city book tour was arranged with national TV and radio appearances and plenty of book signings. It was time for me to step into the spotlight. This transformation happened well before I met Brian. It was too bad the book tour didn't train me to be a great wife and partner. It was a decision I first had to learn to make.

Love Is a Decision

In a Ted Talk, University of Houston research professor Brené Brown makes a claim that vulnerability is the only way to create intimacy. "If we are going to find our way back to each other, vulnerability is going to be that path."[3] Indeed, closeness is the foundation for any relationship. But there needs to be a willingness from both sides to be open to that level of intimacy. Love is based on a decision to be extremely vulnerable with another person. Love doesn't happen to you. You choose it.

As a recovering "need to be right" person, I grew up in an era and a home where "being right" was highly valued. From my first days in school, I saw that raising your hand and having the "right" answer meant you were smart. At home "being right" meant being loved for being smart. I was brainwashed into believing that when I was "right," I was good enough to be loved. Quite the ego boost! But that was about it. It certainly didn't boost my long-term confidence.

As I grew up and matured, I found out there is something so much more important than being "right." It's being "loved." I discovered that when I was committed to being "right," it always meant making someone else "wrong." As you know, feeling wrong does not go well with feeling loved.

Relationship expert and soul sister Heide Banks was pondering an old fight she had had with her now ex-husband after she asked him to buy her some iron supplements at the drugstore and he forgot. She mentioned it to her friend Nat, when she was asking him why he thought she was having such a difficult time with relationships.

Nat said, "One word: liquid iron."

Heide replied, "That's two words."

"Exactly!" said Nat.

In that moment, Nat pointed out to Heide that her need to be "right" was getting in the way of her desire to be loved.

"I think that was the last time I corrected a man," Heide shared.

Since that time, Heide is now happily in love with her soulmate and having the time of her life.

So many of us like to assume a rigid stance and "dig in our heels" to fight for our point of view and prove how "right" we are—often about some pretty stupid stuff. The cost of needing to be right is hurting, harassing, or humiliating the ones we claim to love the most.

Over the years I have finally learned to manage my mind and my mouth. I've learned that most of the time it's not necessary to "correct" anyone on what I think is right or wrong unless it's really pertinent to someone's well-being. Now when I am about to blurt out something in order to be "right," I catch myself, slap some imaginary masking tape over my mouth, and choose love instead.

Deciding to Love Is an Action

All major appliances, cars, and electronic gadgets come with an owner's manual. Often, it's a step-by-step guide that tells us how to turn it on, turn it off, and how to fix it when it's broken. Imagine if your soulmate came with such a manual, the complete guide to the lifetime care and operation of the one you love, a guide that told you how, when, and where to make all your soulmate's dreams come true.

Many years ago I was sitting in a personal-growth weekend workshop when the instructor, Herb, began to share a story about his new wife, Elizabeth. Elizabeth is a woman to whom the little details mean a lot. You can totally make her day by giving her a greeting card embellished with words of love and appreciation. However, Herb, who was madly in love with Elizabeth, just wasn't quite getting it. He was sure she was perfectly happy "knowing and hearing" how much he loved her, but for Elizabeth "knowing" wasn't the same as "seeing."

So out of sheer frustration, she wrote a little "owner's manual," so that he would have explicit instructions on how to keep her smiling. Elizabeth not only wanted lots of love notes, love letters, and greeting cards; she also had specific requests for the kinds of flowers and gifts she desired to receive. Herb didn't really understand "what all the fuss was about," but he was thrilled to have directions. In his desire to keep his bride deliriously happy, he began to shower Elizabeth with notes, cards, and small gifts. As a result, Elizabeth got what she needed to feel loved, cherished, and adored. This was more than thirty years ago, and they are still happily married.

When I initially heard this story, I had a lightbulb moment and thought that every relationship needs this kind of "owner's manual." I tracked down Elizabeth and suggested that she create it as a book. She suggested that we do it together. At that point in my life I was single and had never considered writing a book, but I was so enamored with the idea that I said yes; as a corporate publicist, writing came easily to me. To make a long story short, in 1992 we wrote the book, received an offer from a publisher, and then decided to self-publish *The Owner's Manual: The Fast, Fun and Easy Way to Knowing and Understanding Your Lover*.[4] I quickly taught myself how to market a book, and the book became a success that launched me into a new career as a book publicist and a literary agent.

Why was the book a success? Because it gave couples a safe way to share all the little things in life that were important to them. It gave them a way to understand each other's needs in an entirely different way. It didn't matter if you had been married for ten minutes or ten years. Sharing this information became a way to learn about each other's wants, needs, desires, and fantasies.

Learning to Speak the Same Love Language

We all express and receive love messages differently. Figuring out how you and your partner experience love can help tremendously in strengthening your relationship. My favorite book on this topic comes from Gary Chapman, *The 5 Love Languages: The Secret to Love That Lasts*.

After forty years as a marriage and family counselor, Dr. Chapman had heard a lot of couples' complaints. From these complaints he began to see a pattern. What he was hearing were the same stories over and over again. When he reviewed more than a decade's worth of notes, he realized that what couples really wanted from each other fell into five distinct categories:

1. Words of Affirmation: compliments or words of encouragement

2. Quality Time: a partner's undivided attention

3. Receiving Gifts: symbols of love such as flowers or chocolates

4. Acts of Service: setting the table, walking the dog, or doing other small jobs

5. Physical Touch: having sex, holding hands, kissing

According to the concept, the way you *feel* loved is also the way you *show* love.

Figuring out your partner's primary love language requires you listen carefully, to both positive responses and complaints. In the case of Elizabeth, she was perfectly clear about what she wanted and needed from Herb. She wasn't afraid to ask for it. Even though Herb was telling her on a daily basis how much he loved her and how beautiful she was, she remained frustrated and "unloved," because he had never given her love notes, cards, and gifts. It wasn't until she shared her needs with him that he began to understand how she best received love. Clearly, Elizabeth's number one love language is Receiving Gifts.

Herb's number one love language is Words of Affirmation. How do we know that? Because that is what he continually offered Elizabeth. He offered words of love, because it is what he most needed.

When I first read this beautiful book, I took the quiz and discovered my number one and number two were tied: I am a Words of Affirmation and Physical Touch gal. My husband Brian's two forms of love are Words of Affirmation and Quality Time. Even if you and your partner have completely different love languages, you can learn to speak your partner's love language. Quite simply, you have a particular way you experience love. Because you can only truly receive love that way, you are likely to give love that way too. Yet you can learn to give love in other ways, ways that can be better received by your partner because of your partner's own love language. Learning how you and your partner experience love is the bridge to both giving and receiving it fully. Through conscious decision making, you can choose to speak your partner's language every day. It is one of the fastest methods to bring you closer together. (Dr. Chapman offers a free and easy quiz to determine your love language at www.5lovelanguages.com.)

Another one of Dr. Chapman's concepts that I find really useful is "filling the love tank." The "love tank" is Chapman's metaphor for how much love each person is feeling.

> The soul is a part of us that never dies. It's who we are at our core. And it carries all the messages and the lessons that we've learned in the past, and will carry all the lessons and the messages that we will carry into the future.
>
> *Debbie Ford*

He suggests that you ask each other, "On a scale of one to ten, how full is your love tank?" If your partner's love tank isn't full, then ask how you might be able to fill it. My friend Jack Canfield, coauthor of *Chicken Soup for the Soul,* has another way of asking his wife, Inga, this question. Every week he asks her, "What can I do to make your life better?"

Finding ways to express our love for our partners so that they can not only accept, but also *hear* what you are saying builds the bridge of understanding. Misunderstandings arise when we speak a different language to one another. Identifying how your partner best experiences love along with the willingness to learn and then speak your partner's love language will create an unshakable bond of trust and intimacy.

Sometimes we need an interpreter to understand the other person's language. As we have seen in Chapter 2, men and women often speak a different language. And each person, whether male or female, has his or her own preference in demonstrating and receiving love. How we receive love and experience safety is greatly shaped by belief systems we bring into the relationship.

Listening to the Shadow

Have you ever listened to someone complain about another person? The very things that annoy us about other people are the things we fear in ourselves. Carefully observe your own reaction the next time your partner does something that bothers you. What is it exactly? How does it make you feel? Identify that feeling, because it is your shadow talking.

My late sister, Debbie Ford, was a pioneer in the field of teaching people about their "shadow side" or "dark side," the parts of ourselves we would rather ignore and pretend don't exist. It's the part of every human that formed long ago and contains all the parts of ourselves we have tried to hide or deny, the parts we believe are not acceptable to our loved one, family, friends, and, most important, ourselves. It is made up of everything that annoys, horrifies, or disgusts us about *other* people or about ourselves. As the great Swiss psychologist C. G. Jung says, our shadow is the person we would rather not be.

Debbie devoted her life to showing us how to unconceal our shadow self, to seek and find the gifts in the behaviors and emotions of the shadow, and to embrace what she called "the gold in the dark." She was a *New York Times* bestselling author of books such as *The Dark Side of the Light Chasers, The Shadow Effect,* and her last book, *Courage.* She was also a teacher who deeply knew and believed that inside every one of us is a human being who has the power to be our teacher, our trainer, and our guide, leading us to strength, creativity, brilliance, and happiness. But if the shadow is ignored and left unexamined, this part of ourselves has the power to sabotage our lives, destroy our relationships, kill our spirit, and keep us from fulfilling our dreams.

From its invisible home deep within our psyche, the shadow wields enormous power over our lives. It determines what we can and cannot do and what we will be irresistibly drawn toward. It dictates our attractions and our repulsions and determines who and what we will love and what we will judge and criticize. Our shadow controls how much success we're entitled to create or how much failure we're doomed to experience. The shadow is an oracle that predicts all of our behaviors, driving the way we treat those around us—and the way we treat ourselves.

But our shadow can only wield its power over us when we keep it in the dark. Instead of something to be denied, feared, or rejected, the shadow has our most treasured gifts: the essence of who we are. When we bring light to the darkness, we find the fundamental parts of our true self buried inside—our greatness, our compassion, our authenticity. And as we explore this part of ourselves we most feared, we become free—free to experience the full range of our humanness, free to bask in our glorious totality, free to choose what we do in this world. Our shadow delivers us the blessing of our entire self.

When we make peace with our shadow, our lives are transformed. We no longer have to pretend to be someone we're not. We no longer have to prove we're good enough. We no longer have to live in fear. Instead, as we find the gifts of our shadow and revel in all the glory of our true self, we finally find the freedom to create the life we have always desired.

When it comes to love, marriage, and our most intimate relationships, Debbie taught that our beloved becomes our best "mirror" for dredging up and reflecting back to us the core issues and wounds we most need to heal. In an interview we did together several years ago, she explained it this way:

> We are set up to attract to us exactly what we need in order to be whole again. Every person who comes into our life is a mirror, a reflection of our inner self. And what I can accept about myself, I will be able to accept in my partner. When I have compassion for myself, I will have compassion for my partner. If I can respect myself and my differences with them, I can also respect them. The most amazing thing about shadow work is that when you alter your inner world and learn to embrace, love and have compassion for your shadow, the people around you will also change.

One of the examples she discussed is the very common and often contentious issue of money. The classic pairing of a "spender" and a "saver" remains to this day the number one cited cause for divorce.

Debbie and I were raised in a home where the lack of money was always an issue, and our parents seemed to have daily arguments about it. As we grew up, we developed very different money styles. I became a "saver," and Debbie became a "spender." My relationship to money stemmed from a deep fear that I would someday end up as a "bag lady," because I was programmed to both desire money and fear it. To counteract my fear, I obsessively paid my bills early and never carried any credit-card debt. I only bought clothes and home furnishings that were on sale. If there was something special that I wanted to do or have, such as a vacation or a new car, I saved up for it. I became inordinately proud of my stellar credit rating and developed a sense of financial security.

Until I got married, I had no idea how big an issue money could become in a relationship. Money was definitely one of my biggest "shadows," and it soon became clear it was something I needed to heal.

Brian was raised in a home where there was always more than enough money. He himself achieved his own financial success early in his career. I was fascinated—and sometimes a little scared—by his ease with money. Brian is a friendly, gregarious, and very generous man. He always takes great pleasure in taking our friends out to dinner and picking up the tab for everyone. When his money and my money became "our" money, I often found myself silently judging his largesse. Even though we were fortunate enough to be able to afford picking up the check, in my "poverty-conscious" mind the proper thing to do would have been to equally split the check, unless it was a birthday or some special occasion.

One day I asked him why he was always Quick Draw McGraw whenever the dinner check arrived. At first the question puzzled him, and then he simply said, "It makes my heart sing and, more important, I believe that money is energy and that the generosity of spirit comes back to us in many different ways."

Healing my shadow issue of poverty consciousness and the fear of becoming a bag lady was an inside job that I clearly needed to pursue. In Debbie's lexicon, I needed to find the gift of this particular shadow. As I engaged myself in a deep inquiry about it, I was able to see that the biggest gift of my money shadow was my ambition and solid work ethic. In my quest to never be poor again, I created a very successful career and was careful with the money I earned. I slowly learned to manage the thoughts and emotions I had about money, which required reprogramming myself to really know and believe that I live in an abundant Universe.

The other part of this process required that I be open and vulnerable with Brian about my past pain caused by the issue of money. I needed to explain to him that I come from a long line of those who had deep fears about never having enough. By being willing to share my truth and express my fears and concerns as well as say what I needed to feel safe and secure, I was able to heal my wounds, overcome my poverty consciousness, and let go of my judgments about how Brian spent money. Does he still like to pick up the check? Yes, he does. And how do I feel about that now? It's fine by me. I see the joy it gives him. But I am pleased to announce that Brian has also learned how to shop sales, something he had never previously done!

We all have many stories that inform our choices and behavior, especially when it comes to our intimate relationships. Oftentimes we forget how much personal decision power we have in what we believe, see, think, and feel. When we begin to realize that these stories are running our lives, and not always in a way that serves us, we can consciously decide to change our story, as Brian and I did with our relationship to money.

My friend Jill Mangino found herself in a precarious position three years into her engagement with her fiancé, Ray. With all of her heart, Jill desperately wanted Ray to be "The One," but there were major obstacles in her way. Jill's story was that her perfect mate would share her love of yoga, meditation, spirituality, and all things organic, including her vegetarianism. Ray is a duck-hunting, meat-eating, motorcycle-riding, cigarette-smoking "guy's guy" who is also socially phobic and prefers to stay at home most of the time. Although she had fallen in love with Ray, she was also operating according to her big story that she was the "consciously evolved one" in the relationship and found herself constantly judging his habits, hobbies, and behaviors. Jill's story led her to break up with Ray, telling him that she needed to find someone with whom she had more in common.

"If this is what you need to do, I will accept your decision, but I will wait for you, no matter how long it takes," Ray explained to her, even though she was breaking his heart.

During this time they continued to live together as roommates, because neither of them could afford to sell the house they shared. Ray treated Jill as he always had, with deep care, respect, and love. He even nursed her through an exceptionally bad bout of the flu.

Jill had always fancied herself a true nature lover, gardening and composting to her heart's delight, but one afternoon when Ray returned home from hunting, he shared with her his experience of reverence for the beauty of the woods, the sky, the smells, and the silence he experienced. In astonishment, she saw something that surprised her and really opened up her heart—there are so many different and beautiful ways to commune with nature, not just her way!

A few days later Ray asked Jill to go with him to the funeral of his former boss, Bob. More than 350 bikers were in attendance, but none of Ray's former colleagues would stand up to pay tribute to Bob. Ray put his fears aside, walked calmly to the front of the chapel, and shared from his heart what a well-loved and good man Bob was. It was at this moment, as Jill sat mesmerized, watching him overcome his social phobia, one of the things she judged most harshly about him, that she fell in love with Ray all over again. His ability to speak from his heart and comfort Bob's family made her discover a new level of respect for Ray. She had never felt more proud of him.

Jill realized that her story that she was the more consciously evolved one in the relationship had turned into a form of spiritual arrogance. By being willing to open her eyes and ears and witness Ray's consistent kindness, authenticity, and compassion, Jill came to understand that Ray possessed all the qualities she considered "spiritual."

Finally, after years of an on-again, off-again engagement, she has rewritten her story about Ray and is ready to set a wedding date. Today she lovingly refers to Ray as her soulmate and "personal guru" and couldn't imagine life without him. By changing her story, Jill created a shift in perception that has now positively altered the course of their relationship and the direction of her life.

Note that throughout Jill's entire journey to acceptance and understanding, Ray did not change. Her story about him did. Jill altered her belief that her perfect partner would be "spiritual" the same way she was. What changed was a widening of her perception of human character and spirituality to include those forms that Ray possessed.

Storytelling is a powerful tool that can either create or destroy relationships. When Jill changed her story about who her perfect mate was, she was able to see that she already had what she had been looking for.

The Story Worth Telling

According to a story in the *Journal of Family Psychology*, researchers did a study with fifty-two married couples to discover how they shared the story of how they met, including their initial impressions of each other. What they found is absolutely fascinating. Based on the way a couple shared their "origin of relationship story," the researchers were able to predict, with 94 percent accuracy, whether the marriage would remain stable or end in divorce.[5]

It didn't matter how, when, or where they met. Whether it was seeing each other across a crowded room and love at first sight or a simple introduction through friends at a party, the actual details of the meeting became insignificant. What did make a big difference was the energy, enthusiasm, and expressiveness with which they shared their story. The couples who shared their story in a negative or withdrawn manner tended to split within three years of getting married, while the couples who shared their story with fondness and nostalgia stayed together.

"How did you two meet?" is a question Brian loves to ask when we are out with a new couple. He is always genuinely interested in all aspects of their coming together. And of course once we hear their story, they generally want to hear our story and will ask me to share it with them. Admittedly, we have a pretty awesome tale to share. It's a wild and lengthy story full of magic, miracles, synchronicities, and blessings from an Indian holy woman. One of the most unusual things about our meeting was that before we met, each of us had dreamed of the other. In my dreams I received clues that would let me know he was "The One." Brian actually saw my face in his dreams!

I have told this story thousands of times. Quite honestly, I sometimes get tired of hearing myself tell it. Oftentimes Brian pipes in to remind me of bits and pieces of the story that I am forgetting or leaving out. On an intuitive level I have always known that sharing our soulmate story reinforces the love and devotion we have for each other and, although I might resist telling it, by the time I am done sharing I feel excited and reinspired.

As an exercise to reinvigorate the story of your meeting, try this. The next time you and your partner are spending time with another married couple, ask them to share their story with you. Chances are they will ask to hear your story. Plan ahead to have an awesome story to share and then tell it with high energy and great detail, adding in all the little things that will be sure to put a big smile on your mate's face. Include items such as:

- Your first positive impression of him

- The body part of his you found most attractive

- Something funny or kind that you observed him doing

- Any feelings you had that he might be "The One"

- Positive reactions from family or friends when they first met him

- How you felt when he first kissed you

Sharing positive stories about your mate will reinforce sweet feelings, put him in a good light, and create even more love in your relationship. Shifting perspective by emphasizing your mate's positive attributes not only alters the energy within you, but between you too.

FOUR

Sacred Contracts and the Dwelling Place of the Soul

To be fully seen by somebody, then, and be
loved anyhow—this is a human offering that
can border on miraculous.

Elizabeth Gilbert

No one likes difficult situations. And yet life seems to toss us a pile of challenges we think we shouldn't have to deal with.

What if I were to tell you your life wouldn't be the same without these challenges? I don't mean your life would be better. I mean it wouldn't be the life you were meant to live. Through my various spiritual experiences, I have come to realize our lives unfold according to both a plan we made before our lives began and the consequences stemming from our ability to exercise free will in every moment. Challenges come in many forms. Whether it is a major tragedy such as bankruptcy, unemployment, illness, a fatal accident, or homelessness or more minor ones such as lost mail, malfunctioning gadgets, misbehaving children, or burned toast, our lives are filled with milestones and obstacles. Each one of us has our prescribed list of challenges we are meant to face.

If you think of your life as a movie, you are actually following a prewritten script that began well before you were a twinkle in your parents' eyes. The accumulation of lifetimes brings you back to learn more lessons. Karma, the residue of learning that has yet to take place, follows you through each cycle.

Like a film producer, you selected the protagonists you would interact with well before coming onto the movie set. In other words, you held a casting call for each and every potential player before you were born to ensure your next life would be spent working off the karma that is yours alone.

As in any movie, you have poetic license. One actor might choose to respond in one way, while another may choose a completely different approach. The movie may run shorter or longer, depending on whether you cut out scenes or put in new ones. You have an enormous amount of choice. In fact, we all make choices based on our current level of awareness.

Karmic connections with other people are a given. If you pay close attention to the most intense situations in your life that bring both joy and sorrow, you will begin to see the drama of your karmic buildup unfolding and working itself out.

Have you ever met someone for the very first time, but you got the feeling you have known this person "all your life"? Well, you may have just met the person in this form, but you have known him or her in other lifetimes. You recognize the person's soul, an energy that is indestructible.

Most likely, your romantic partner is one of the key soul players in your movie. He plays a pivotal role in bringing up all your internal junk. Whether you like it or not, he is a significant member of your cast. As infuriating as he may be, your anger is yours alone. He is not to blame, nor are you. He is merely pointing out what is inside of you, and you are reacting to it.

It doesn't mean his behavior is legitimate or kind or praiseworthy. But if it is having such a negative impact on you, it is important to ask yourself why. What does it trigger within you? If you can identify the originating moment of the pain—meaning the first time you felt that particular emotion—you will realize that it has nothing to do with your partner at all. His behavior serves merely as a reminder of how you felt that emotion for the first time.

If you can accept that all emotion resides within yourself, you can begin to take ownership of your feelings. No one can make you feel a certain way. Happiness and hate begin—and end—with you.

Naturally, how you decide to deal with the challenges you face is entirely up to you. Although you have a prewritten script, you have the freedom to change its direction, pace, and tone. You can opt to focus on one character or group of characters more than others. You can even change the ending. The impact from the choices you make is never quite clear until the film has been made. Hollywood film creators will tell you they have no idea how the entire project will turn out. They trust their instincts, choose the best collaborators possible, and hope for the best. Life is a bit like that too.

If you consider the karmic connections we have with people, the challenges we face make a lot more sense. Have you ever wondered why you continuously struggle with the same issues, regardless of the people you interact with?

Sacred Contracts

What if I were to tell you those interactions are based on a sacred contract you made before you were born? If you begin to think of your life as a movie with your very own beginning, middle, and end, you will see that everything happens for a reason. Whether it is the loss of a love or the loss of a job, our life lessons shape us for a specific purpose. If you don't believe me, consider the following story.

It was raining. I was cranky. Quite simply, I wasn't in the mood for bad news. Yet there I was, sitting in my astrologist's office, listening to the worst astrological reading of my life.

The bearer of the "bad news" was a beautiful woman in Los Angeles named Linda, who was both an astrologer and a spiritual counselor. She had informed me that the planets were currently aligned in my chart in "deep winter." I had arranged for a reading because my life was already depressing and challenging, and now she was assuring me more of the same for the coming six months.

It was 1991, and my corporate public-relations business was suffering the consequences of a major recession. Eight-five percent of my business evaporated in a one-month period. I had gone from a staff of eight and four thousand square feet of prime office space in Beverly Hills to an office the size of a closet with one part-time

> The soul is the fingerprint of God that becomes the physical body, unique in its own development and expression, but filled with the divinity that is the essence of all that is.
>
> *Iyanla Vanzant*

employee. I had no idea what to do next and was considering a total career change. On top of my professional challenges, my two-year relationship had just ended abruptly, and I was also suffering from exhaustion with Epstein-Barr syndrome. It was a triple whammy that sent me reeling.

She also told me that I would meet my soulmate within the year, but that he was already married. However, we would work together for many years and would build healing centers. I am sure that somewhere in this reading Linda attempted to soften the blow and convince me that there was a rainbow with a pot of gold at the end of it, but in that moment all I could hear was, "More trouble coming—run and hide."

As I was writing her a check for the session, she began to tell me that her mother had recently died. During her morning meditation that day, she had had an extraordinary experience that she felt compelled to share with me.

Linda confessed that she and her mother had always had a difficult relationship. In Linda's view, her mother had been unkind, critical, judgmental, and completely unable to give Linda the feeling of being loved and cherished. A longtime spiritual seeker, Linda often felt guilty that, in spite of her years of study and meditation practice, she couldn't find a way to forgive her mom or heal their relationship.

As she sat in meditation, she clearly saw and heard her mother, who looked better than she had in years. Her mother apologized to her for her behavior and then explained to Linda that the two of them had been together before in many life-times and had played many roles with each other. Before they reincarnated for this life, Linda had asked her to assist her in taking a serious approach with her spiritual growth. Together they decided that having a "difficult" mother would be the best path for Linda's evolution. As Linda listened to her mother speaking, she began to "remember" this agreement and could feel the healing of her heart as she realized there was nothing to forgive for either of them. They had agreed from the start that their relationship should take this path.

Hearing Linda's story was a revelation for me. Suddenly I could see that the tough times and difficult people in my life just might be happening for a reason. Chances are I had even "asked" for these experiences!

Before you start rolling your eyes, consider how many people have been in your life who have taught you hard lessons you would not have otherwise learned. Difficult situations teach us infinitely more than easy ones.

Although I was still anxious about the prospect of another six months of "deep winter," I left Linda's office with a tinge of excitement and a ton of curiosity about how and why life is the way it is. Could it be possible that the challenges I faced were actually gifts in disguise?

During the next six months I was obsessed with figuring out my future. I had given up on re-creating the previous way of earning a living, but was baffled about what my "life purpose" was. As I looked back on all the clients I had lost, I had to admit to myself that, although I had made a lot of money, I didn't enjoy the hard-core business clients I was serving. I decided that if I was going to continue being a publicist, I would only represent people, places, and things that were making a positive impact on the planet. This new level of awareness allowed me to form a new mission statement. At the time I didn't have a clue about what my new role would look like, but on a soul level it felt right.

One day in 1992 my friend Patrick Netter and I went out to lunch. As we ate chicken salad at a Sunset Boulevard outdoor café, I told him about my new career direction. He asked me a life-changing question: "If you could represent anyone in the world, who would it be?"

Without batting an eye, I instantly said to him, "Oh, it's someone you probably have never heard of. His name is Deepak Chopra."

Patrick's eyes lit up as he laughed heartily. "Not only do I know who he is, but my good friend Penny works for him. If you want, I can connect you to her and maybe she can arrange a meeting."

Being a woman of action, I spoke to Penny later that day. She told me that Deepak was indeed in search of a publicist. Because he happened to be in Los Angeles the following week, she could set up a meeting.

I had seen Deepak speak on several occasions. He had an impressive ability to explain the medical reasons behind the mind-body-spirit connection. His work affirmed everything Louise Hay had shared in her books, but he was able to explain things from a scientific perspective.

He was twenty minutes late for our meeting. When he walked into the room, he apologized for his tardiness and explained that he only had five minutes before his next appointment.

I just smiled and said, "That's okay. I only need two minutes. If you are as smart as I think you are, you will hire me to be your publicist."

He looked at me for a long beat, laughed, and said, "Okay, let's do it!"

That was the start of a twelve-year working relationship. From the very beginning, it felt as though we had always known each other. A few years later he told me he believes that I was his sister in a past life.

One evening, before I took him to a TV appearance, we had dinner together at an Indian restaurant. We sat at a window seat overlooking Wilshire Boulevard. I asked him if life is pre-destined or if we have free will. I will never forget his response.

"It's both, depending on your level of consciousness."

I was still thinking about Linda's interaction with her mother and wondering about how much of life was predestined and if we actually had much control over our lives. I was especially in-trigued with the idea of these past-life agreements. I could see how we might have *both* agreements with family, friends, and events *and* the free will to honor or not honor the agreements.

The level of ease and compatibility I felt with Deepak led me to believe that we had an agreement for this lifetime. Intui-tively it felt right. One of the first big projects we worked on to-gether was the opening of the first Chopra Center in San Diego, a healing center that provides Ayurvedic health treatments, meditation classes, and a wide array of spiritual studies.

Linda had been right. I did meet a soulmate: Deepak. He was married to Rita, who was clearly his romantic soulmate. Be-cause she accepted me into the family right away, I came to see how we were all soulmates of the friendship kind. The most mind-blowing piece for me was that I came to understand that a soulmate is not just a "one and only" romantic partner; we can have many soulmates and on many different levels of relationship.

It became clear to me that we do indeed make agreements with certain people before we incarnate. So-called sacred contracts, these agreements serve the purpose of guiding us toward our personal development and empowerment and making a contribution to the soul of humanity.

Caroline Myss wrote a powerful book on this topic entitled *Sacred Contracts: Awakening Your Divine Potential*. She says: "The contracts and negotiations your soul has made, in my opinion, form the texture of your life. You make arrangements for certain commitments, for opportunities to meet certain people, to be certain places, but what you do and how you are when you get there, that's where choice comes in."

As I emerged from my "deep winter," my new mission statement materialized. Along with my new client, Deepak Chopra, I was now working with Marianne Williamson, Wayne Dyer, Joan Borysenko, Louise Hay, Neale Donald Walsch, and many others. The demand for my time expanded rapidly, and I was fortunate enough to be able to choose whom I wanted to promote. I came to rely on my intuition to guide me, welcoming clients with whom I had sacred contracts.

In order to fulfill our destiny, we need to recognize our soul tribe and the interconnected sacred contracts that bind us.

Sometimes those contracts end within our lifetime. Sometimes they begin later in our lives too.

Soulmates with an Expiration Date

In 1967, Susie McCall, a twenty-year-old in a small town in southern Ohio, had big dreams to finish college and become a high-school English teacher. Cute and bubbly, Susie made friends easily. Her favorite pastimes were reading and playing music, and she was head over heels for her boyfriend, Terry, whom she had met a year earlier when he asked her for a ride to their hometown. Although the relationship was far from perfect, Susie loved that he expanded her interests, especially by introducing her to the art world, and considered him her soulmate. But because his habit of being a bit aloof and not always emotionally available made her nervous and uncertain, she sometimes wondered if they really had a future together.

A year and a half into the relationship, her destiny took a sudden new trajectory when she discovered she was pregnant. A shotgun wedding was planned, and on March 16, 1968, Susie and Terry married. The wedding was a small, lovely affair in the local church in which she grew up, with her sister and cousins as bridesmaids. Even though her parents and close family members were very disappointed that she "had" to get married, her mom made her wedding dress, and all put on a gracious, happy face for the big day.

As she walked down the aisle, two months pregnant, Susie was both excited and scared about her future, but she hoped for the best. After the birth of their daughter and even though their new marriage was rocky, Susie didn't allow herself to question whether to stay or go in her marriage, although doubt kept nagging at the edges of her mind. Like all couples they had their ups and downs, and their biggest problems revolved around communication and emotional honesty. In spite of it all, Susie was committed to sticking it out and making it work.

"It wasn't horrible, but my marriage really did fall short of what my hopes and dreams were. Often I felt that we were meant to be together, that there was some kind of karma that was at work. I consciously made the decision to love him and keep our family together," Susie explains.

"The truth is, I was too scared to even think about the possibility of leaving and finding a new soulmate," says Susie, so she stayed even though she wanted somebody or something different. She actually didn't want somebody else—she wanted her husband to be someone different from the person he wanted to be.

When they reached the benchmark of their thirtieth anniversary and their daughter was now grown, she and Terry both realized that the relationship was over, and they came to a mutual decision to divorce. Susie realized that although she still loved him, they wanted very different things from life and she could no longer be with him. Their mutual interest in sailing that was the glue that held them together simply wasn't enough anymore. But they remained friends, and she still views him as a soulmate.

Several years before her divorce, Susie was in a car accident that necessitated chiropractic treatments. Her chiropractor was also a metaphysical teacher who held weekly classes at his office. It was at these classes that she met Otto Collins, who was recently divorced and also a victim of a car accident. Less than a year after Otto began attending these classes, they had a "soulmate experience" that totally rocked their world, and they fell in love.

For the past eighteen years they have been blissfully in love and have become love experts and coaches. Because they began their relationship knowing that their soulmate experience wasn't enough to create lasting love, they knew they had to learn how to communicate, love one another even when it was difficult, and keep their passion alive—things they hadn't done in their previous marriages.

About two years into their new relationship, people started asking them to give talks, presentations, and seminars about their secrets to attracting and keeping new love. It was what they learned from their own relationship as well as various training sessions that they've lovingly shared with the world since 1999 through their coaching, websites, books, and courses.

Today Susie realizes that her life path, including her previous marriage, was perfect, even though it didn't feel that way when they were separating. She says, "I believe that my ex and I came into this life with a sacred contract to marry and raise our daughter. On our honeymoon, I started spotting and later was told that I could have very easily lost our daughter, so I absolutely know that our little family was meant to be—and she stubbornly wanted to come and be with us."

"If I had left the marriage several years earlier," she continues, "then Otto and I wouldn't have been together. It's very clear to me that our coming together was a situation of divine timing for both of us. The many years I spent with my ex-husband were essential to my growth and preparation for the amazing relationship I have today with Otto."

What Is the Soul and Where Does It Live?

Rabbi Yanki Tauber, of Chabad.org, offers a wonderful definition of the soul:

> The soul is the self, the "I" that inhabits the body and acts through it. Without the soul, the body is like a light bulb without electricity, a computer without the software, a space suit with no astronaut inside. With the introduction of the soul, the body acquires life, sight and hearing, thought and speech, intelligence and emotions, will and desire, personality and identity.

In truth, not just the human being, but also every created entity possesses a "soul." Animals have souls, as do plants and even inanimate objects; every blade of grass has a soul, and every grain of sand. Not only life, but also existence requires a soul to sustain it—a "spark of G-dliness" that perpetually imbues its object with being and significance. A soul is not just the engine of life; it also embodies the *why* of a thing's existence, its meaning and purpose. It is a thing's "inner identity," its raison d'être. Just like the "soul" of a musical composition is the composer's vision that energizes and gives life to the notes played in a musical composition—the actual notes are like the body expressing the vision and feeling of the soul within them. Each soul is the expression of G-d's intent and vision in creating that particular being.[6]

I believe that when two souls are meant to come together, there is a vibrational recognition that can't be denied. Just six weeks after we first met, Brian and I took our very first trip together to Yosemite National Park. We biked and hiked through the majestic mountains and stunning valleys, talking nonstop about every topic imaginable. It was as if we needed to catch up on the decades of life experiences we had already lived. From mundane things like favorite books, films, and food to esoteric religions and philosophy, we discovered that we shared a vast array of interests. Like most couples newly in love, we were living in a delicious world that was part magic and part dopamine. Quite simply, we were in sync, and it felt like the greatest high imaginable.

From Yosemite we traveled to San Francisco and checked into a quirky and charming boutique hotel off Union Square known as the Monaco. Our room, although quite small, was beautiful, a jewel box of vibrant colors and unique design.

I remember waking up the next day to the soft morning light pushing quietly through the blinds and illuminating Brian's face. He was smiling. Suddenly I felt an intense wave of anger rush over me, and with the anger came a vivid memory. It was no longer September 1997, but a time that felt like two thousand years ago. Cold waves of loneliness and devastation gripped my body, because my husband of that time had left me, yet again, for a religious mission. Before I could really even process what I was seeing and feeling, Brian stopped smiling as he looked deep into my eyes and said, "I will not leave you in this lifetime. I promise."

He had spoken the unspeakable. Shocked that he knew that I was having this incredibly strange and unusual experience, I asked, "How did you know?"

Brian explained to me that part of the reason we had come back together in this lifetime was to heal each other. Obviously, this feeling of abandonment was one of the wounds in need of healing. He said that in at least two prior lifetimes he had abandoned me for religious missions and that he would never do it again.

Stop the presses! Are you kidding me? This was one of the strangest moments of my life. Although I had considered the possibility that we had been together in past lives, I hadn't spent any time thinking about it. As a generally pragmatic person, I am much more interested in what is going on right now in present time than what may or may not have happened long ago in a past life.

At the same time, I couldn't deny that this extraordinary incident was a turning point for me. It made me aware that one of the benefits of finding your soulmate is the healing it generates not only for wounds from this lifetime, but also for those from past ones. I began to comprehend that our soulmate is also our teacher, and lessons will be pleasurable, painful, and all points in between. In that moment in the precious light of that San Franciscan morning, I realized that a soulmate is like a karma coach. He or she accompanies us on our journey to wholeness, completing past experiences in this lifetime and beyond.

Those of us who believe in karma, reincarnation, and the afterlife understand that one of the core reasons we incarnate into a physical body on earth is to undergo life lessons for our personal evolution and growth. Quite often, these are lessons that require interactions with other souls we have traveled through eternity with, also known as our soul tribe or cluster group. Our tribe is made up of old friends and family who have approximately the same awareness level. Many times our "soulmate" is part of this group. Michael Newton, an expert on the topic of reincarnation and the author of *Journey of Souls,* explains it this way: "Members of the same cluster group are closely united for all eternity."

We choose to come back into physical form to work through karma and lessons. Before being reborn, we go through an intense planning process on the other side where we consult with our "guides" and various members of our soul tribe to make decisions about who will play what role in our next life. Newton uses the analogy that life is one big stage play and we have the lead role as actor or actress. We also select other characters to appear in our play with us and are, in turn, selected by other actors to play parts in their productions.

A soulmate is one of the most important characters to cast in our new life. A soulmate becomes our designated companion, and we agree to help each other accomplish mutual goals. These soulmate relationships are *designed* to come with karmic lessons. Some of these lessons will be ecstatic, and some will be brutally painful. This is normal! Chances are you have spent many earthly lifetimes with your soulmate and, as in all relationships, there were major highs and major lows. Together you each acquired some karmic debt with the other.

Newton explains that in order for soulmates to "recognize" each other on the earth plane, a wonderful and mysterious process, they attend "classes" known as "the place of recognition." When you and your soulmate are in the "place of recognition," you agree to create some signs, symbols, déjà vu feelings, or synchronicities that will occur when you meet on the physical plane, so that you will be sure to "recognize" each other. At the moment of your birth, there is a spiritual amnesia that takes place and you conveniently forget all of this!

I once did a session with a past-life regressionist who took me to the place "in between lives." I saw a very vivid scenario of myself standing—or what you might consider floating—in dark space looking down onto a large black glass table. On my right side was my father and on my left side was my sister, and all three of us were connected by a few brightly colored luminous cords of light. Together we were selecting the woman who would be a mother to me and Debbie and a wife to our dad. We jointly decided on a woman who was completely new to our soul tribe. Debbie and I selected her for her brains and long legs. Dad selected her for her beauty. This was the only thing I can remember from this session.

However, when I decided to consciously manifest my soulmate, one of the things I created was a "soulmate wish list" of the traits and heart qualities I desired my soulmate to possess. The only physical trait on this list was that my soulmate would have gray hair. This was something that I was completely certain of. He had to have gray hair.

On the day that Brian and I met, the first thing I noticed was his gray hair—he had gone gray in his thirties! It was a clue; it was probably something we had arranged when we were in the "place of recognition." That day we also had many other clues and synchronicities, which was fortunate for me. Without the clues I might have missed him, as he wasn't, upon first glance, "my type."

Sometimes it takes a crystal ball to know whether the person right in front of us is destined to be our soulmate. Although we may think that soulmate connections should be filled with magical flow, ease, and grace, opposition inevitably arises. The confusing part is how insistent the Universe can be when two people are meant to be together, even when the odds are not in their favor.

Back to Eden

The story of Donna and David, as illustrated in their book *The Energies of Love: Using Energy Medicine to Keep Your Relationship Thriving,* shows the sometimes circuitous route soulmates take to get to one another.[7]

When Donna Eden first saw David Feinstein, before he had even looked her way, she distinctly heard words that told of a deep and profound love, including—and she remembers this verbatim—"This man will spend the rest of his life with you." Did Donna's hearing this establish them as *soulmates*? Was it the fulfillment of the promise that "some enchanted evening, you may see a stranger . . . across a crowded room"? Popular literature about soulmates suggests a feeling that with your soulmate you are entirely whole, healed, and intact, like no piece is missing from the puzzle, punctuated with flashbacks to past lives together; a profound wordless understanding of one another; an easy acceptance of one another's flaws; and a reliable sense of security in one another's presence. That's not quite how it happened for this couple, or anyone else they knew, for that matter. In their early years together, they had to fight for every last shred of compatibility.

Nonetheless, their partnership also seemed to have a fated quality to it. That kept them together for several years, but eventually they ended their relationship and went their separate ways, living hundreds of miles apart from one another. Having undergone a very painful grieving process about the end of the relationship, Donna was finally feeling free in her heart to welcome whatever was to be next in her life. She spent some time on a mountain in Oregon savoring the feeling.

As she was driving down the mountain, feeling joyful and triumphant, she heard the same voice that she heard on the night she had met David. It was as clear as if it were coming out of the radio in her car: "Despite appearances, you will marry the man."

Having just gone through the agonies of getting "the man" out of her system, she was furious and started to argue. She was living in Ashland, Oregon, and David was still in San Diego, where they had met. There was no likely way they were going to be running into one another. It was over, and she mentally but emphatically stated this fact.

"You will be spending the summer in San Diego," said the voice.

"That's ridiculous!" Donna's mind replied. "Besides, how would I support myself and the girls?"

Undaunted, the voice replied, "Jobs will be coming!"

That week Donna received in the mail offers to teach seven separate classes in San Diego during the following summer. Meanwhile, one of her closest friends in San Diego called her to suggest they swap houses, as she wanted to spend the summer in Ashland. Now all her reasons not to make the visit to San Diego had dissolved.

Donna called David to inform him that she was going to be spending the summer in San Diego. She courteously told him that she wanted him to learn about this directly from her rather than through the grapevine, and she wanted to assure him that she was not coming back to reconnect with him in any way. Weeks went by after Donna returned to San Diego without their seeing one another. In fact, David had already become involved in another relationship.

Then on June 21, 1981, in San Diego, four years to the day after they first met, David pulled into a gas station. As he stepped out of his car, he couldn't believe his eyes. There stood Donna

Eden, pumping gas! When their eyes met, a wave of electricity went through them both. David almost screamed at her, "No! We can't do this. I'm practically married." His protests were, however, no match for the energies that were magnetically drawing them toward one another. After only half an hour of talking, their relationship was firmly, irrevocably reestablished.

When David got home, the woman he had just started living with was packing her stuff. She prophetically said, "I don't know what's going on, but I think you need some space."

Another interesting coincidence is that when David had pulled into the gas station, he was returning from a visit with his parents. As he was leaving, his father said, "I have a book for you. It's one that shaped a lot of my thinking about health back in the 1940s, and I just found an extra copy that I must have picked up somewhere along the way." The name of the book was *Back to Eden*.

Before all of that, while trying to reconcile the deep connection they felt with how damn hard it was to be together, David brought their birth information to an astrologer. The astrologer told him, in essence, to find somebody else; there was no way this relationship could flourish. Feeling quite silly about resorting to something as unscientific as astrology, he at least wanted to see if there was agreement among different astrologers. He took the same birth information to two other astrologers who came to virtually the same conclusion. Donna was already living in Ashland at the time, and David decided to make one last visit to be sure that it was really unworkable.

Meanwhile, Donna had befriended a woman, Kate Maloney, who had a local reputation for being a remarkably gifted astrologer with profound spiritual depth. Donna arranged for them both to have a reading with her. On the appointed day, however, Kate called Donna and told her that she had been sick and had not been able to do the joint chart. David was on his way back to San Diego the next day, so they never had that reading. While their time together in Ashland was actually quite profound, David decided that their shared history had been filled with so much strife, combined with the negative portents of the three astrologers, that it just wasn't the right path for him to pick up and move to Ashland. He ended their relationship with a phone call that was agonizing for them both.

A few days later, Kate called Donna and told her she had completed the chart. Donna told her it was too late. She didn't want to see all that she sensed was right about the relationship now that it was over. The next morning, Kate called again and said she had just had a dream that she believed was telling her that Donna should come in for the reading. Donna still wasn't interested. A couple of days later, Kate called yet again and said that her "guides" were on her case to get the information to Donna. Donna still wasn't interested. About that time, David and Donna had a phone conversation to tie up some loose ends. In passing, Donna mentioned the astrologer's persistent attempts to share her interpretation of their joint chart. David, believing that the reading would corroborate the strikingly similar conclusions of the other three astrologers and thus make it easier for Donna to let go of their relationship, encouraged her to make the appointment.

When Donna went in, Kate described a profound harmony that was more important than the surface incompatibilities reported by the other three astrologers. Kate also saw what the others were focusing on, but she felt there was a deeper story. She said, "You will not be having children together [they were both still in their thirties at the time], but your family will be the 'family of man.'" David, a psychologist, and Donna, an energy healer, were both in private practice, and they had no ambition back then to work together or expand beyond their own individual practices. In the end, however, they joined forces and, over time, began to collaborate, blending their respective disciplines and talents. By the time of this writing, they have reached close to half a million people with their classes and books, and they have trained and certified more than a thousand health-care practitioners who are offering services to untold numbers of people every week. Providing healing for the "family of man" was to become the defining purpose of their lives.

Despite the seemingly mystical synchronicities that brought Donna and David together, they are the first to affirm that their relationship is just like everyone else's. They still get irritated with one another and miss one another's signals in ways that can be inconvenient and downright hurtful. So are they soulmates with a clear destiny together or just another couple inching their way forward day by day?

After long careers in helping people live in greater alignment with their highest potential—what Abraham Lincoln referred to as "the better angels of our nature"—Donna and David believe that human destiny is determined by three essential factors: choice, fate, and chance. The choices you make every day are the most decisive ways you shape your future.

The role of fate in your destiny is most obvious in your genetic inheritance. Your height, natural aptitudes, and vulnerability to certain illnesses—although they may each be mediated by your choices and your circumstances—are, to a considerable degree, determined by fate. Fate also selects your family and the conditions that shape your identity and personality. Beyond simple genetic inheritance and family and culture of origin, the concept of fate also implies that certain other circumstances in your life are also predestined.

How might that work? Just as the structure of a maturing body is inherent in the energies that surround the embryo, as was persuasively demonstrated by Harold Saxton Burr in his work on bioelectrodynamics, each of us carries an energy that may influence key events in predetermined ways. Even occurrences that appear to happen by chance may be orchestrated by the invisible hand of fate.

Some things, however, appear to be the products of pure chance, such as which people are injured in an earthquake or other mass disaster. On the positive and creative side, the Universe utilizes chance, down to random genetic mutations, as the engine of evolution and expansion.

All three—choice, fate, and chance—play a role in all people's lives. Whatever combination of choice, fate, and chance brought you together, your relationship is a journey of your souls, a meeting of the deepest sources of your being. As French philosopher Pierre Teilhard de Chardin said, "We are not human beings having a spiritual experience, but rather spiritual beings having a human experience." In this sense, the term "soulmates" is useful as a constant reminder that more is going on between you than what is obvious and at the surface.

The term is not useful, however, if you take "soulmate" to mean that in order for your relationship to be spiritually valid, it somehow has to embody the qualities of ease and sense of destiny mentioned earlier. That concept does not provide a realistic set of standards against which your relationship can be measured. When you come together, your souls are mutually creating a new story on earth that is influenced by the older stories that propel each of you forward. The choice is not whether your relationship is a journey of your souls, but how much you let that dimension of your partnership into your consciousness and mindfully foster it.

Soulful Synchronicity

My friends Lana Love and David Almeida both experienced synchronicities that brought them together. Lana is a divorced psychotherapist and energy healer in Australia. She was hell-bent on manifesting her soulmate; she actively went to singles events and committed to using the Law of Attraction to bring her beloved to her. On her soulmate wish list she stated that she wanted to be with a "mystic author." One night she decided to Google the term "mystic author." She discovered an American named David.

She soon found David on Facebook and they began exchanging posts, which led to e-mailing, texting, and Skyping each other. They had great conversations about the meaning of life and the state of the world. Out of these conversations a friendship began to emerge, which later deepened into a love relationship. After visiting Lana in Australia for just five short days, David moved in with her and her two daughters. Today they are soulmates, lovers, best friends, and business partners. They have a successful radio show called *Universal Soul Love,* where they discuss issues that involve consciously creating the New Earth Paradigm.[8]

Both Lana and David fulfill each other's needs. Since he came into her life, Lana has been able to heal the grief and trauma of abandonment she felt from both her father and her first husband. The greatest gift David has given her is the support she has needed to apply her own talents. She has a successful radio show, is writing a book, and runs a successful business, all of which were made possible through David's presence in her life. Her dream of having extensive connections and being able to empower and influence others is now coming true because of their relationship. Before she met David, she was a single mom with few resources to accomplish her goals. Now she is fulfilling her greatest mission.

As a former private detective, David had to solve every type of case imaginable. As a result, he honed his skills as a problem solver. Part of his life's mission is to support women and their feminine essence. He had been married for twenty years, but after his father died, he received a wake-up call asking him if he really wanted to live out the rest of his life the way it was going. He yearned for new challenges and recognized his relationship in his first marriage had a natural expiration date. Raising two children in a foreign country while building a new business was just the challenge he needed. Through these opportunities, he has experienced a lot of spiritual and personal growth. Lana has shown him a deeper love than he had ever experienced before, which has brought a lot of healing into his life.

A *Gift from* The Secret

Healing is something we do for each other, even if it often looks as though we are simply digging deep into past wounds like a kid shoveling sand in a sandbox. Lynn and Bob's story is a perfect example of how hardship can make our relationships rock solid.

As a little girl Lynn Rose was captivated by Cinderella and all the many fairy tales about magic and princesses. She dreamed of meeting her own prince someday, fully expecting that the arrival of her prince would set off an explosion of fireworks. She envisioned that their meeting would be a deep, spiritual, and soulful "rising to the heavens" experience. And, of course, they would live happily ever after because that's what princes and princesses do.

She never imagined that it would take her fifty years to find her soulmate and that he would arrive emotionally and financially broken.

A well-known and much-loved inspirational speaker and singer-songwriter, Lynn is a tall, gorgeous blonde with a wide circle of friends in the personal-growth movement. Having done a variety of emotional development work on herself, she was aware that her childhood traumas caused by her alcoholic father and judgmental mother were standing in the way of a deep, lasting intimate relationship. Her biggest issues revolved around perfectionism and a fear of being controlled and "taken over."

One winter evening in 2006, as she sat on her couch with her laptop, she began to watch the film *The Secret,* which features an array of Law of Attraction experts explaining how to make your life's dreams come true. When Bob Doyle appeared on the screen, she remembers feeling as if she had been "punched in the gut." "I found myself listening intently to every word he spoke, and I instantly felt as if we had known each other across time. I even had a flash of us being together in this lifetime," she recalls.

With a little searching online, Lynn soon discovered that Bob was married with children and promptly decided to forget him.

Many months later, Lynn was scheduled to host the red carpet interviews and sing at a charity gala. When she finally had time for dinner, she discovered she hadn't been assigned to a table. Scanning the room, she spotted an opening at a table that had one available seat. As she sat down and glanced across the candlelit table, she saw Bob Doyle sitting directly across from her, talking to one of her friends. She was startled by his appearance. The handsome, vibrant man from *The Secret* was barely recognizable. He looked troubled, tense, and uptight. In spite of that, she instantly felt a strong pull toward him and an inexplicably intense chemistry when they briefly spoke, which she kept to herself.

What she didn't know was that Bob was in marriage hell. He and his wife of more than twenty-four years had tried repeatedly through the years to "save" their marriage and in the process managed to have a third child, but things had been rapidly going downhill.

The following year at the same gala, Lynn and Bob met in person again. This time they had a longer conversation. They talked about the possibility of doing some kind of a joint business project together. The day after the gala they collaborated on a short video, and even though she again felt the chemistry with him, neither one of them acknowledged it.

Bob went back to the East Coast, while Lynn remained in Los Angeles. At this time, they began to speak regularly. They continued their conversations about collaborative business ventures, but as they got to know each other better, Bob eventually opened up and shared about his life and deteriorating marriage.

During this time Lynn began to suspect that Bob might be her soulmate and was amazed at the level of shared interest and connections they had, but she didn't want to do or say anything to break up Bob's family. In fact, she encouraged him to get help to be sure he'd done everything he could before he chose to leave.

Eventually Bob realized that what would ultimately be best for him, his wife, and the children was to follow through with the divorce in spite of his misgivings about leaving his children. He'd attempted leaving numerous times over the past decade, but this time he stuck with his decision.

One month after officially leaving the marriage, Bob went to Los Angeles for an event and called Lynn to meet up with her while there. Bob was living through high drama with his wife at the time, feeling stressed to the max, scared, and shut down. During this time Lynn was experiencing her own upheavals as well. Despite the conflicts in both their lives, that chemistry, that bond was undeniably there. From that moment forward, their friendship shifted to a romantic connection. Things went swiftly from there—perhaps too swiftly.

"Three weeks after Bob had arrived in LA, now two months after he'd just left the marriage, he practically moved in with me, as he'd been crushed financially and needed to not spend money on a place to stay. We were both in our own survival mode at the time, and yet it felt like the right thing to do. It's a crazy way to start a relationship. We never got to have a court-ship or a honeymoon phase."

Relying heavily on her intuition that Bob was indeed her soulmate and that someday they would find their way to be-ing truly happy together, Lynn became the strong one, shoul-dering the financial burden, becoming head cheerleader for Team Lynn & Bob, and helping him rebuild his confidence. Lynn admits that her fantasy of "being taken care of" was far from being realized during her initial time with Bob. "When I would question myself and wonder if I was just mislead-ing myself," she says, "I would sometimes have to rely on my 'deepest knowing' and a 'constant choosing' to get through the next hour, day, week, or month, constantly choosing unconditional love and trust."

During the next two years they built a solid relationship and a business together and have become instruments of growth and expansion for each other. Bob's brilliance in technology and his fame from being on *The Secret* combined with Lynn's knowledge of the media, marketing, and client care contributed to their success.

It took them six months of stress-filled working around the clock to reach the income level they needed and desired. Maintaining the business took its toll over the long run, but it also provided the stability they needed to then transition into honoring their real passions by partnering in a healing music brand. As a result, they have finally regained their sense of balance—financially as well as emotionally—and created a brand that has a positive impact on the world that could only have come through their particular collaboration.

In their personal lives, Lynn's love of life and enthusiastic way of being in the world lit up the dark cloud hanging around Bob from years of feeling shut down in his previous marriage. Lynn's compassion and acceptance of Bob's challenges and stress gave Bob the freedom to move through that unbearable time to a place where he is now thriving.

"If anything, we feel like we've done it backwards," Lynn says. "We were thrown into the fire from the beginning, weathered all kinds of storms, and had to stand the test of time and challenges. Now we can relax into the bond of the relationship itself. Most relationships start out like a fantasy and then get tested when challenges hit. We've reversed how that played out and are far stronger for it. I now know that a soulmate is a partner who is there as a mirror for us to fully grow and discover who we are, who we can be, and who we are meant to be."

Today they are 100 percent there for each other. As best friends, lovers, and business partners, they are committed life partners who love each other unconditionally with honesty, implicit trust, and open communication. They even both believe they have been together in past lives.

"In spite of the phenomenal difficulties and pain we went through initially, we have finally begun the 'honeymoon' phase. It was worth all we've had to withstand, and we are both grateful for the gifts of profound growth we experienced as a result, along with how we've come together to uniquely contribute to the world as a couple," Lynn concludes.

Soulful relationships deepen our experience of one another. But as with any relationship, soulmate relationships are not any easier. The good news is they connect us in powerful ways that can help when things get tough.

FIVE

Irreconcilable Differences Are Normal

Your task is not to seek for love, but merely to seek and find all the barriers within yourself that you have built against it.

Marriage is like a marathon. To be a marathon runner it takes constant effort to stay in form. The night before the big race you experience excitement, anticipation, and maybe even a little fear. Your monkey mind might be filled with thoughts such as: Can I really do this? Did I train hard enough? Will I make it to the finish line? When I hit the "wall," will I have the inner strength and commitment to push through?

The night before the wedding, most first-time brides are looking forward to their "princess moment," and if they are possibly feeling last-minute stress, it is about the food, the flowers, or whether crazy Uncle Joey is going to be drunk before dinner is served. Their preparation for the event has mainly focused on the details of the occasion, picking out the right wedding dress, sending out the invitations, registering for gifts, and planning a memorable honeymoon.

The difference between brides and runners can be summed up in this way. Nearly all runners spend months, if not years, getting into shape and training for the marathon. They are not casually signing up for a twenty-six-mile stroll in the park. They know they need to prepare, both physically and mentally, for this grueling endurance event.

Imagine if part of the prewedding preparation included becoming a "student of love"! The truth is not many people think of the marriage as they prepare to marry. But how can they? First-time married couples lack the context or experience to understand what they are entering into. Most people can't get past the wedding itself. Relationships would benefit greatly from a shift away from just preparing for "The Big Day" toward preparing for "A Big Life—Together."

Here's the good news: it's not too late to make a commitment to "train" for a lifetime of love and joy in your relationship.

One of the most liberating and shocking marriage facts I have ever heard came from University of Washington psychologist and researcher Dr. John Gottman, who discovered that all couples have at least *nine* irreconcilable differences. These are "unresolvable" issues that are often the source of arguments. Below I have listed ten of the most common ones:

> In-laws and extended family involvement
>
> Balance between home and work

Communication

Sex

Personal habits and idiosyncrasies

Sharing household responsibilities

Outside friendships

Political views

Money and debt

Disciplining children

Let's look at an example of how one couple managed their differences involving money.

Having met Denis in her forties, Peggy McColl was accustomed to taking care of her financial responsibilities on her own. Her successful business earned her a very healthy income. Sure, being an entrepreneur involves financial risk, but her belief system was based on trust and an appropriate commitment to fulfilling her financial obligations with ease and harmony. In short, she had an attitude of financial abundance, not one of fear or lack.

A cautious person by nature, Denis had been trained as a military pilot who never stepped aboard a plane without a backup plan. What he perceived as smart thinking landed on

Peggy's ears as negativity. She emphasized possibility; he emphasized caution.

Peggy's interpretation of his probing questions about money was that he didn't trust or believe in her. On some level, she felt attacked and surprised by his relentlessness about financial matters.

Over dinner one evening, she decided to get to the bottom of it all. Gently broaching the subject, Peggy asked Denis why he was so concerned about money, since they were both doing well financially. Denis revealed that in his previous marriage his wife had been very irresponsible with money. He described how she once spent twice her salary in a year, heaping a substantial financial burden on their already wavering relationship. Her reckless spending habits created severe tension in their marriage, something he never wanted to repeat. Since Denis was trained to have a backup plan, he needed some reassurance that everything would be fine in the event that, due to an accident or illness, Peggy couldn't earn an income. His biggest apprehension was that he would have to carry the entire financial burden if she wasn't able to contribute. His concern didn't stem from distrust or a lack of belief in Peggy's business decisions; he simply needed assurances that things were in place to give him peace of mind.

As she mulled over their conversation, Peggy had a tremendous realization a few nights later. Snuggling on the couch while watching a televised hockey game and enjoying their favorite pizza, Peggy suddenly realized that their combined points of view on handling money offered them something of incredible value: long-term security and peace of mind. She saw that her positive attitude toward always having an abundance of money meshed beautifully with Denis's caution. He not only had a plan A; he also had a plan B. He was trained and prepared in the event of unexpected challenges.

Two great things came from the couple's money *differences:* respect and a long-term vision. When Peggy realized the origin of Denis's cautiousness about money, she purchased three types of insurance and made some investments to provide a greater safety net. She also learned to respect Denis's own beliefs about money without trying to convert him to her way of thinking.

Imagine knowing, before you were married, that there would be a long list of important issues upon which you and your mate will never agree—or will actively disagree—for some time. Now imagine understanding that this is normal and that what is called for is learning the skills and tools to love, respect, and thrive in spite of what looks to be chaos and breakdown!

One thing Brian and I decided to do early on in our relationship was to make a decision that our union would be our number one priority. We promised one another that our choices would be based not on what Arielle wanted or what Brian wanted, but on what was ultimately best for our relationship. This shared commitment meant that when we encountered the inevitable disagreements and upsets, no one would threaten to walk out, and both of us would take responsibility for finding a solution.

Learning how to discuss issues with your partner starts with kindness, respect, and affection. Research has shown that 96 percent of the time, the most important part of a potentially difficult dialogue with your partner is the first three minutes. Those first few minutes predict how the remainder of the conversation will go. By deciding in advance that you want to approach your partner with kindness, respect, affection, and maybe even some humor, you will guarantee a greater chance of a happy outcome.

Gottman believes that, when discussing differences, it's imperative to avoid what he names the "Four Horsemen of the Apocalypse":

1. Criticism (attacking your partner's character)

2. Contempt (conveying disgust, the number one factor that tears couples apart)

3. Defensiveness (blaming and counterattacking your partner's character)

4. Stonewalling (disengaging or deliberately ignoring your partner)

Remember to bring up issues gently and calmly use "I" statements rather than accusatory, critical, or sarcastic statements. Don't blame and shame, but rather speak for yourself. For instance, you might say: "I felt unappreciated and ignored at dinner last night when we were with the Smiths," or "I feel unsupported when I share my need for more help with my current projects."

If you are the one listening to your partner's "I" statements, remember not to exhibit any of the Four Horsemen of the Apocalypse behaviors, but rather turn toward the person physically and ask in a loving, caring tone of voice: "Tell me more. I want to understand and make this right for us."

In 1990 Gottman did a study with 130 newlywed couples at a retreat and then followed up with them six years later. One of his biggest discoveries was that turning toward your partner, or responding to what he calls a "bid," is a great indicator of a successful marriage. All day long our partners make requests for connection. Brian often wants to share with me items he reads in newspapers and magazines that he enjoys and thinks I will find interesting as well. Although I often have other things I am doing, I stop, take his "bid," and look at what he has offered. Ninety-nine out of a hundred times he is right; I do find these things interesting. If I were to ignore him or turn away, he would perceive that as a sign of disinterest.

Six years after his retreat with the honeymooners, Gottman found that the couples who were still married had a "turn toward the bid" 87 percent of the time. Nine times out of ten, they met their partner's emotional needs. Conversely, couples who had since divorced or were in chronically unhappy marriages had a "turn toward the bid" of only 33 percent. He calls those who succeeded in marriage "masters" and those who failed "disasters."

"There's a habit of mind that the masters have, which is this: they are scanning their social environment for things they can appreciate and say thank you for. They are building this culture of respect and appreciation very purposefully. Disasters are scanning the social environment for partners' mistakes," explains Gottman.[9] Masters create a climate of trust and intimacy while disasters create a climate of criticism and contempt. Quite simply, masters are looking for what's right, while disasters are looking for what's wrong.

Kindness as a Muscle

We know that contempt and criticism kill romance and marriages. The antidote is practicing kindness. Kindness has been shown to be one of the greatest indicators for long-term happiness in a relationship. Think of kindness as the superglue for love.

Being kind does not mean being nice and pretending you don't feel the way you do. Being kind means being authentic. You still get to express your anger and hurt, but it is the way in which you show your emotions that matters. Instead of blaming the other person, explain why you are hurt or angry. That is the kinder path.

If kindness doesn't come naturally for you, remember to just practice it as if you were building a new muscle. When you feel yourself starting to blame, show contempt, criticize, become defensive, or turn a cold shoulder, take one physical step back, breathe, and count to ten. The more aware we become of our knee-jerk responses, the sooner we can read the signals we are sending and the quicker we can alter our behavior the next time.

We Have to Talk

Creating the climate for a loving, respectful, and kind conversation does not occur when someone begins by saying, "We have to talk!" in a threatening tone of voice. Except for perhaps hearing from your doctor, "You have cancer," the words "We have to talk" are probably one of the scariest things a person can say to another. When your buttons have been pressed and you are in emotional turmoil, effective communication can only follow if you calm yourself down and get centered and clear. At the end of this chapter I will provide several effective emotional release tools that I frequently use.

Harville Hendrix says that the number one quality of a great marriage is safety. We must feel physically and emotionally safe with our partner as well as connected and passionate. When we feel safe with our partner, we can drop our defenses and feel our sense of connection to each other. And with this comes a sense of joyful and relaxed aliveness.

He also says that all criticism is "a form of violence." "Whether criticism is phrased in a gentle way or a cruel way, it comes from a place of judgment," Harville explains. He recommends that all couples take a sacred oath of zero negativity: Zero negativity is when both parties "commit absolutely to refraining from put-downs, negative comments, and behaviors. It's imperative that both members of a couple make a strict commitment to this approach. Not just temporarily, but always."

Asking for this kind of commitment can be as easy as saying to your partner, "You know, baby, I just really love how you do A, B, and C for me and our family. You are just the best when it comes to D and E. And I want us to continue to grow together and have a dream relationship, one where we both always feel emotionally safe. The other day I heard about the Zero Negativity Pledge, where we agree to never put each other down or make negative comments to each other. I would love it if we could agree to do this with each other. What do you think?"

If you get some resistance from your partner because he feels he needs to occasionally give you some "feedback," ask him if he would be willing to do it in a kinder, gentler way and in a warmer tone of voice. Your partner may not change immediately, but if you find yourself being criticized, you can respond in a neutral voice, "Would you be willing to say that to me in a different way?" Zero negativity doesn't mean that you can't or don't ask for changes in behavior or that you suppress your concerns or desires; it's all about the way the asking is done.

Generally nonconfrontational, I am a wimp when it comes to "serious conversations." If my husband and I do have to have a "talk," I am always hoping to get it over as quickly as possible, whereas Brian is quite comfortable exploring issues from every angle. Unlike me, he has the curiosity and stamina to talk for hours and, in some cases, even days.

Despite our differences, which you might say are rather irreconcilable, we have discovered over the years that one thing that can build the bridge between breakdown and breakthrough is communication. Thanks to our experience with so many great experts on communication, we have learned a secret I want to pass on to you: timing is everything.

Imagine trying to build the city of Rome while you really have other projects to finish first. It creates tension when you are pulled in various directions. If you have something important to share with your partner, you don't want to try to off-load your thoughts when he is busy, stressed out, or otherwise distracted.

How will you know when the timing is right? Ask. The simple words, "Is now a good time for a short conversation? There's something I'm having a hard time with that I need to share with you" are one way to open the subject. If "now" isn't a good time, ask him to let you know when he is available.

Before you get to the heart of the matter, remember to frame your thoughts first with expressions of love and appreciation. Start from that place in your heart. Be willing to be vulnerable and talk in "I" statements in a warm tone, without being accusatory.

Try to keep the conversation short, no more than thirty minutes (ten minutes is ideal for most men) and if you do need more time, take a break and then come back. These discussions aren't a win-or-lose competition. Think about it. How can you win when the person you love most in the world is losing?

Another important consideration when having difficult conversations is the setting in which you have them. Brian and I often have our chats when we go out for a walk. I've heard that for some couples being in the car and driving makes it easier and more conducive. By having important conversations while taking a walk or a long drive, instead of having a serious sit-down, knee-to-knee encounter, you are not creating the environment of "we are now working on the relationship." According to love experts Gay and Kathlyn Hendricks, this more casual setting "frees up creative energy," and if you are talking while walking, "you're pumping blood and oxygen through your body and brain instead of sitting on your bottom." As Kathlyn likes to say, "If it's physical, it's therapy!"

Wherever and whenever you decide to have that heart-to-heart talk, remember that you are a team seeking to solve an issue as a win/win for the relationship and commit to doing it with love, respect, and kindness.

How to Listen When Your Partner Needs to Talk

One of the best ways to carefully listen so your partner feels certain that you are "getting him" is to learn a simple and easy five-step technique known as the Imago Dialogue:

STEP 1: *Listen* without interrupting.

STEP 2: *Act as a mirror.* When your partner stops talking, repeat back to him what you heard as accurately as possible. Ask, "Did I get that?" and "Is there more?"

STEP 3: *Summarize,* especially if he added "more." Then ask again, "Did I get it all?"

STEP 4: *Validate.* "What you said makes sense to me." This statement doesn't mean you agree with him; it simply lets him know you understand.

STEP 5: *Empathize.* Let him know that you can imagine, if you were in his position, how he might be feeling, such as hurt, scared, angry, disappointed, and so on.

When you listen in this careful, structured way, your partner will feel seen, heard, and understood.

By now you have received several tools to improve communication. But what if you are at the breaking point, overwhelmed with emotion and unable to speak properly? Managing emotional turmoil is an important skill that will improve not only your quality of life, but also the quality of your relationships. Over the years I have created an emotional toolkit to help me fine-tune my mood when I'm feeling stressed, anxious, or simply out of alignment with myself and my surroundings. Here are several effective emotional release tools that I've found effective.

Tapping

The first method involves a self-soothing technique known as EFT tapping, which stands for Emotional Freedom Technique tapping. Having used this method daily for years, I have been able to release many kinds of emotional turbulence, physical pain, and even writer's block! Backed by research, this effective technique involves using your fingers to lightly tap on acupressure points on the head, body, and hands. Millions of people have found it to be an effective form of therapy for anxiety, depression, anger, post-traumatic stress disorder, and so much more.

My dear friend Nick Ortner is a world-renowned expert on tapping and the bestselling author of *The Tapping Solution*. Below is a step-by-step guide to use when you are afraid or anxious about having a serious talk with your mate.

In this tapping technique you will be releasing internal blocks to improved communication in a relationship. Even when we want to improve communication in a relationship, whether with our spouse, mom, child, friend, or neighbor, we still often experience internal resistance. There are a lot of different reasons that we may resist the idea of opening up to someone in a relationship. There may have been a breach of trust at some point or we may have experienced negative reactions in the past that made us feel unsafe when we were open and vulnerable. We may have also been taught that expressing emotion, which is a necessary part of improved communication in relationships, is unacceptable or inappropriate in some way.

> The soul is the core of your being. It is eternal. It doesn't exist in space/time, a field of infinite possibility and infinite creativity. It is your internal reference point with which you should always be in touch.
>
> *Deepak Chopra*

Whatever the case, in order to improve communication in a relationship, we first need to address our own internal blockages to being more open with that particular person. This exercise is meant to serve as a guide to get you tapping on this topic and give you some general language for and ideas on how to tap.

As always, if the language doesn't apply to you, you can change it to fit your needs. As you go through the exercise, notice any specific ideas, thoughts, impressions, emotions, or memories that you can use to tap on either during this session or on your own. The more specific you can be with your particular experience, what you're feeling exactly, what happened, what you believe, the better your results are going to be.

Before you begin tapping, it's best to rate yourself on a scale of 0 to 10, in which 10 means you are in extreme emotional discomfort. This way, after each round of tapping you can determine your progress, so that eventually you will reduce the discomfort down to a 1 or 2 or even zero.

TAPPING TECHNIQUE

First, spend a few minutes doing what I call "negative" or "truth" tapping. Tap an area or two while expressing what you're currently feeling. The purpose is not to anchor it in, but rather to acknowledge it and let it go. Feeling safe to acknowledge how you feel and to speak the truth about your current experience is one of the most powerful things you can do.

Next, focus on one relationship in which you want to improve communication. Visualize yourself openly expressing to that person how you feel. In this visualization, you will share more of yourself and life with that person.

Do that now and notice how it feels. How uncomfortable and unsafe does it feel opening up to that person? Are you

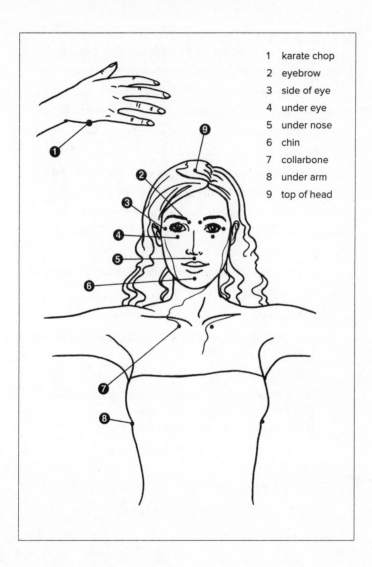

1 karate chop
2 eyebrow
3 side of eye
4 under eye
5 under nose
6 chin
7 collarbone
8 under arm
9 top of head

willing to be that open and honest, even without knowing what kind of reaction you will get? See that now and focus on that feeling. What comes up? What do you feel in your body when you see yourself opening up? On a scale of 0 to 10, how uncomfortable do you feel about opening up in this particular relationship?

Now take three deep breaths in as you begin to feel safe and grounded in your body. Become present in time and space. Feel the feelings about opening up to someone else. Now we will start by tapping three times on the karate chop point.

As you tap on each of the body parts listed below, repeat the corresponding phrases.

Side of hand:

"Even though I am really uncomfortable being open and honest with this person . . ."

"I love myself and accept how I feel."

"Even though being more open in my communication with this person feels way too risky . . ."

"I love myself and accept how I feel."

"Even though opening up with this person feels like a really bad idea . . ."

"I deeply and completely love and accept myself."

Eyebrow: "I just can't open up to this person."

Side of eye: "It doesn't feel safe."

Under eye: "I don't know how the person will react."

Under nose: "I don't think I can be more open and honest with this person."

Chin: "I might get hurt."

Collarbone: "I might hurt the person."

Under arm: "It's just not a good idea."

Top of head: "It just doesn't feel safe to be more open with this person."

Eyebrow: "I am not sure I can do it."

Side of eye: "What if someone gets hurt?"

Under eye: "It doesn't seem like a good idea."

Under nose: "It is so hard to trust this person with my feelings."

Chin: "I just don't want to do it."

Collarbone: "But if I don't open up, things might never change."

Under arm: "Our relationship might never improve."

Top of head: "And this relationship is so important to me."

Eyebrow: "I want this relationship to improve."

Side of eye: "And that might mean I need to open up."

Under eye: "I need to be willing to communicate."

Under nose: "That may mean taking some risks."

Chin: "It might not feel safe."

Collarbone: "And that's okay."

Under arm: "I acknowledge the parts of me that don't feel safe."

Top of head: "Opening up."

Eyebrow: "What if I could just get started?"

Side of eye: "I don't have to do it all at once."

Under eye: "I can start by being a little more open with this person."

Under nose: "Little by little I can share more about how I am feeling."

Chin: "And that is still scary."

Collarbone: "And that's okay."

Under arm: "Because what's more scary is not trying to improve our communication."

Top of head: "It's time to make this change now."

Keep tapping through the points at your own pace, moving through eyebrow, side of the eye, under the eye, and so on, and feel the feelings in your body. See yourself talking to this person. Visualize it now. What is it you need to say? See yourself saying it. How do you feel when you say it? Is there tension or fear in your body? Just notice those feelings. Tap through the points, and feel as they release. See yourself saying what you need to say. How does the person react? Are you scared of what he or she will say? Are you scared of what might happen? Feel the feelings in your body.

Just keep playing that movie in which you say what you need to say. Feel yourself being grounded, feeling safe, opening your heart, being present in that moment in time, speaking your truth, and doing it with love and compassion. See yourself saying what you need to say. And feel how good it feels in your body to be open, to be loving, and feel that feeling. No matter what the person says or how he or she reacts, you are speaking your truth. And you feel safe in your body doing so.

Run that movie one more time, tapping through the points and feeling more safe each time you do. Release any previous negative experiences, memories, or anything that prevented you from feeling safe communicating. Let go of all these fears. Feel your heart open up again, feeling safe to trust, to communicate, to speak your truth, and feel how good it feels to be strong, to be loving, to be kind. Feel that feeling in your body.

When you're ready, you can gently open your eyes and stop tapping.

Take a deep breath and notice what you're feeling now. Run that movie again. See yourself opening up to that person.

And check in. Does it still feel uncomfortable? Where is the intensity on the 0-to-10 scale? Was it a 10 before, and it's an 8 now? Or a 5? It means you're moving in the right direction, releasing the resistance. What else came up during that process? What other emotions, memories, and ideas?

Take a moment to write down anything else that arose during the exercise. Either continue tapping on it now or commit to addressing it in the future, opening up in a relationship, speaking your truth from a place of love and compassion, which can change everything. Commit to continuing to release any resistance you have about this topic and improving your communication in your relationships.

This method takes a bit of time, but there is a second approach you can take when you notice emotions are starting to bubble up to the surface. It is as simple as dropping a pencil.

The Sedona Method

One of the fastest and most effective emotional-release techniques that I use on a regular basis is the Sedona Method. I had the good fortune to learn it from a master, Hale Dwoskin. Hale was once a client, and I am now happy to call him a friend. As the author of the *New York Times* bestseller *The Sedona Method: Your Key to Lasting Happiness, Success, Peace, and Emotional*

Well-Being, Hale has been helping men and women have happy, healthy, satisfying, and fun relationships for four decades.

The Sedona Method is a simple way to tap into our natural ability to let go of the feelings that stand in the way of our having, being, and doing what we choose. In just seconds you can release anger, hurt, fear, frustration, disappointment, worry, and anxiety. This method is particularly helpful during those times when you just feel like giving up.

The first step in the process is to allow yourself to *honor whatever you are feeling.* Then, allow yourself to simply feel the way you do. For instance, if you have hit "level-ten mad," avoid pretending the anger isn't there or trying to find a way to distract yourself. Instead, give yourself a moment to be where you truly are: level-ten mad.

Next you can *make a choice.* You can choose to stay mad, or you can choose to find out what's really true in your heart. Sometimes our anger is justified and sometimes it's not. Either way, we can learn to let go of the anger and rediscover what's really true for us.

If you decide to discover what's in your heart, the next step is to *recognize that you can let the feeling go.* A good test is to try to maintain that level of anger for five minutes or more. Can you do it? Most likely, you will find yourself thinking about other things in those few minutes of concentration. Anger is exhausting. The good news is that not being able to stay angry is also a sign that you are able to move on, even for a second or two. In just those few minutes, you can prove to yourself that you *can* let things go.

It doesn't matter whether your partner deserves being let off the hook or not. It's your choice and impacts *your* well-being first and foremost. When you choose to let go, you are unhooking the one who is most important: you. Once you do let go, all sorts of new possibilities open up to you.

One of the first times I heard Hale speak before a crowd about the Sedona Method, I found the concept of "letting go" just a bit too vague for me. It sounded way too simple. Just let go? I wasn't sure about it at all.

Then Hale had us do an exercise. We put a pen in our right hand, closed our fist around it with fingers pointing down, and held our right arm out straight. Then Hale instructed us, at the count of three, to simply open our hand and *let go*.

Voilà! I finally got it. Letting go can be that fast and easy.

Here are some simple questions you can use to let go:

1. "Can I let it go?" Dig deep here. Really, can you? If you have ever thrown out the lint from the dryer, then you can also let the bad feeling go too.

2. "Will I let it go?" Herein lies the question of willingness. Would you rather feel unhappy or happy and free for your own peace of mind and clarity?

3. "When will I let it go?" "When" is an invitation to decide to choose to let go and be free now.

These questions may seem simple, and they are. That's why they are so effective. Just like the effective communication exercise in this chapter, the Sedona Method also requires an acceptance of your personal responsibility and your commitment to happiness. Repeat these questions as often as you need to, until you feel the peace of mind, clarity, and happiness that you are looking for. If you apply these questions regularly, you will be able to tap into your intuitive knowingness and make the right decision for you.

Heart Lock-In

The third method in your emotional toolkit is extremely effective in tapping into your feelings of love, appreciation, and gratitude. Once you have cleared your frustration, anger, disappointment, or whatever emotion was getting in the way of having a really loving, open, and successful chat with your beloved, I recommend you do a Heart Lock-In. It is a technique I learned from the HeartMath Institute that allows you to reconnect with your positive emotions.

The heart is a muscle that pumps life-giving blood and oxygen throughout our bodies. We already know that cardio workouts such as running, biking, hiking, and using elliptical machines are proven ways to improve our long-term health and strengthen our hearts. In the same way, a Heart Lock-In improves the emotional and spiritual strength of your heart—only you don't have to break a sweat to reap the benefits!

For the past thirty-five years the visionaries at the Heart-Math Institute, located in Boulder Creek, California, have studied the heart. Their research offers compelling evidence that the heart possesses its own intelligence and has great influence over how the body's many systems align themselves. HeartMath scientists have found that when we focus on the area around the heart while remembering and reexperiencing feelings such as love, appreciation, or gratitude, the positive results can immediately be seen and measured in our heart rhythms, or the so-called heart-rate variability. These heartfelt emotions cause our heart's rhythm to become smooth and ordered. They call this "heart coherence," a highly desirable state that improves our emotional, physical, and spiritual well-being.

Using the HeartMath techniques is one way to begin to feel more love for yourself and your soulmate. Just as your bicep muscles respond to lifting weights on a regular basis, spending time each day focused on the experience of love, appreciation, or gratitude builds a reservoir of these good feelings, which translates into greater love, joy, and harmony in your relationships.

The Heart Lock-In technique takes about five minutes. Make sure you are in a quiet, comfortable space. I find it helpful to close my eyes and breathe slowly and a little deeper than normal. With step 3 I send these feelings of love to myself and to Brian.

Heart Lock-In steps:

STEP 1: Focus your attention in the area of the heart. Imagine your breath is flowing in and out of your heart or chest area. Breathe a little slower and deeper than usual.

STEP 2: Activate and sustain a regenerative feeling such as appreciation, care, or compassion.

STEP 3: Radiate that renewing feeling to yourself and others.

With practice, a Heart Lock-In can provide physical, mental, and spiritual regeneration and resilience. The next time you find yourself dreading something, you can easily perform a Heart Lock-In to manage your emotions about the issue and to work through them at the same time.

For an experience of this, please visit www.matetosoulmate .com/audio for a short process to release annoyances with your partner and become heart-centered again.

SIX

Going from Annoyed to Enjoyed

Love is not finding someone to live with;
it's finding someone you can't live without.

Rafael Ortiz

We are creatures of habit. As we grow up, we learn from our parents the "right" way and the "wrong" way to do things. Eventually we marry and discover that our partner has a completely different way of doing things, and that is when the trouble starts. We bring our assumptions, fantasies, and memories into a marriage with our "right way" and "wrong way" radar on high alert. One of us believes that a towel can be reused for five days; our partner insists on a fresh towel after every shower. One of us believes kitchen countertops are for holding every possible appliance, while our partner believes counters need to be as clean and clear as possible. And let's not even get started about the direction the toilet paper "should" unroll in.

The crazy thing is that most of us never realize that we have the ability to *question* our beliefs and habits. As human beings, we have the magnificent capacity known as *choice*. We can decide at any moment to make new choices about our beliefs, habits, and ways of doing things. But instead of exercising this choice, many of us fault our partners and rapidly slide into judgment, criticism, or resentment.

There is an easy solution to this dilemma. It is something I call Wabi Sabi Love. Wabi Sabi is an ancient Japanese aesthetic that honors all things old, weathered, worn, imperfect, and impermanent. Wabi Sabi seeks beauty in imperfection. For instance, if you had a large vase with a big crack down the middle of it, a Japanese art museum would put the vase on a pedestal and shine a light on the crack. Or it might fill the crack with 24-karat gold!

Wabi Sabi Love is about attaining groundbreaking shifts in perception, so that you can embrace and find the beauty and perfection despite, or perhaps even because of, each other's imperfections. I call this "going from annoyed to enjoyed"!

They say necessity is the mother of invention, and that was exactly what I needed when I found myself, as a first-time bride at forty-four, with no partnership skills. I had been familiar with the concept of Wabi Sabi, but it wasn't until I was married that I thought about expanding the concept and applying it to making a relationship work. After running my own business for many years, I knew how to be the *boss,* but I had no idea how to be a good *partner.*

Brian and I use code names when we start acting annoying or annoyed with one another. We have had many heated mo-

GOING FROM ANNOYED TO ENJOYED

ments when this strategy has worked extremely well. After he's called me Sheila or I've called him Wayne, we usually look at each other and laugh, because we've recognized we've both learned behaviors that shoot us into orbit.

Brian and I agreed that the toilet paper should always roll top down, but when it comes to toothpaste we are on opposite sides of the fence. I am certain that the proper and correct way to handle the tube of toothpaste is to always squeeze from the bottom and then roll the empty part upward, neatly and precisely. My amazing soulmate does it the "wrong" way. He is a "mangled from the middle" squeezer. For our first few years together, I would often ask him, as sweetly as possible, "Honey, could you please squeeze the toothpaste from the bottom . . . the correct way?"

He would look at me as if I were totally out of my mind, shake his head or laugh, and then walk away. It became clear that he had no intention of changing his toothpaste-squeezing ways. Every time I walked into the bathroom and saw my poor mangled tube scrunched up on the counter, I would get a bad feeling in my stomach and think, "Why can't he just do it right?"

I often thought the solution was to buy two tubes of toothpaste, but I realized that even the sight of his mangled tube would bother me. I knew this was a silly thing to be bothered by, and yet at least once a day I was confronted with my annoyance at the mangled tube of toothpaste.

One day I decided to find the Wabi Sabi solution to my dilemma. I placed the tube in the palm of my hand and asked myself, "What's good about this?" The tube just stared at me blankly, offering no answer at all.

Then I prayed and asked God to show me, "What's good about this?" And suddenly, the answer came: "Thank God I married a man who brushes his teeth!"

In a Wabi Sabi God-inspired flash of insight I found the answer. Now every time I see the mangled tube of toothpaste on the bathroom counter, I smile, knowing that I will grow old with a man who may end up with his own teeth because he diligently takes care of them.

Another instance in which I had to whip up some Wabi Sabi Love magic involved Brian's TV viewing habits. My amazing soulmate is a political news junkie. He absolutely loves to be highly informed about what's happening in the world. The upside of this for me is that he is my "in-house" news editor; at the end of my day, he shares with me the most important world happenings. That perk, however, is not enough to offset one very big downside: Brian likes the TV on loud. We are talking really, really loud.

I have an aversion to anything loud.

He also has a habit of turning on the TV in every room he walks into. One day I came home and all four of our TVs were on. And, as he likes it, the volume was cranked up on every one of them. The amazing part was that Brian wasn't even home!

On that day I realized I needed to figure out the Wabi Sabi Love solution to this dilemma, or I would certainly go crazy.

As I mentioned, Brian wasn't home, so I walked around the house, picking up each remote control and turning off all the TVs. When I picked up the fourth and final remote, lightning struck. The solution became crystal clear.

I was never going to change Brian's proclivity for turning up the volume on the TV, but I could take total responsibility for turning off all the "unwatched" TVs. Now whenever Brian and I are watching TV together and he leaves the room, I can (and do) lower the volume. Most of the time he never even notices!

When too many "little things" in a marriage compound, they may eventually add up to that Great Big Thing that will destroy the partnership. Just imagine the possibilities that will open up in your relationship when you learn to accept, embrace, and even find the gift in your partner's perceived imperfections. It's not just about tolerating our partner's so-called flaws, but actually finding the perfection in the imperfections. By learning to live Wabi Sabi Love, you will create a heartfelt, loving, long-lasting, committed, joyful relationship that lights you up as a couple, knowing that you are greater together than apart and that your bond will be forever stronger, deeper, and more meaningful as a result of embracing this practice.

A willingness to embrace even the oddest of discrepancies can forge relationships based on unconditional love.

Who cares if your kitchen floor takes a bit of a beating in the process?

Love Lessons from the Kitchen Floor

Even though Diane truly loved Jerry, she was confronted on a daily basis with something about him she found very hard to embrace: his passion for poppy-seed bagels. Since childhood, Jerry has had a love affair with this particular snack, and in fact he enthusiastically devours one nearly every day. Jerry slices and toasts his bagel and then takes it into his home office to relish its flavor.

But like Hansel in the fairy tale, Jerry always leaves a trail of poppy seeds that leads across the white kitchen floor, through the center of the house, and into his office. Jerry is aware that he is a bit of a "sloppy Joe." Although he often makes an effort to clean up the poppy seeds, his cleaning skills somehow never result in the utterly spotless floor that Diane would like.

One day Diane was feeling uncharacteristically grumpy. When she entered the kitchen, looked down, and found herself skating across a sea of scattered poppy seeds yet again, her level of grumpiness increased a hundredfold. As she had done a thousand times before, Diane moistened a hand towel and got down on her hands and knees to begin cleaning up the mounds of accumulated seeds.

"Just once," she thought, "I would like to come into the kitchen and not find these poppy seeds," huffing as she vigorously hand-wiped the floor to her satisfaction. As she sat back on her heels, a thought struck her through the haze of her own frustration. "What if the floor never had any more poppy seeds on it?"

As if hit by lightning, Diane suddenly realized *that would mean there would be no more Jerry!*

Tears flooded her eyes as she stood up. She gazed down at the few remaining poppy seeds that were gritting up her floor. Instead of looking like grains of gray sand, they suddenly looked amazing to her—like little black diamonds that represented everything in her life that was precious and sacred to her. She rushed into Jerry's office, threw her arms around him, and kissed him through tears of joy. He gave her a quizzical yet loving look as he popped the last bit of poppy-seed bagel into his mouth, then brushed the seeds that had landed on his shirt onto the floor.

Today she describes it this way: "Now no matter how many seeds I may mop up, I'm very peaceful inside. Whenever I see those poppy seeds, they fill me with so much love and gratitude. And on some days I deliberately leave them and my old compulsive behavior behind as I smile, turn on my heel, and walk away."

Diane's tender and beautiful Wabi Sabi Love shift in perception led her to see those pesky poppy seeds as proof that she now has another day to spend with Jerry. Perhaps author and philosopher Sam Keen explained it best when he said: "We come to love not by finding a perfect person, but by learning to see an imperfect person perfectly."

Relationships require us to stretch in unimaginable ways. It happens to everyone, even the president of the United States. No matter what your political views are, the story of Barack and Michelle Obama is another great example of how two people worked through their differences by embracing their individual responsibility to move from being completely annoyed to truly overjoyed.

Personal Responsibility

Over a decade ago Barack and Michelle Obama's marriage was about to crumble. Barack told his grandmother that Michelle's constant nagging was driving him crazy.

Michelle told her mother she wasn't sure their marriage would survive. They were drowning in debt from the Ivy League law-school loans. Michelle was the major breadwinner with her high-profile corporate job. With two young girls to care for, she felt fat, unseen, and unheard. With Barack's busy travel schedule, they barely had any family time. To add to the mix, she was tired of picking up after him.

One day Michelle woke up at five o'clock in the morning. Barack was gently snoring next to her. All she could think about was getting out of bed and going to the gym. It had been months! Part of her resisted going, and her mind began to make up reasons why she shouldn't go. The girls would soon be up and would need to be fed. But another, larger, part of her thought, "Barack's a smart guy. He'll figure out how to feed them." So she pulled herself out of bed and went.

At the gym she got on the StairMaster and promptly had an epiphany. She realized she had been waiting for Barack to make her happy. But as the beads of sweat started to form on her forehead, she realized it was up to her to make herself happy. No one could do it for her.

When she got home, she found Barack and the girls at the breakfast table, where she announced the new rules of the Obama household. First, she was finally going to take her mother's offer to begin helping out with caring for the kids. Second, every night that Barack was in town, the whole family would eat dinner together at six thirty. Third, Sundays were to be family day, no exceptions. And finally, a weekly date night would be put on the calendar.

Today, as we all know, the Obamas have a fabulous relationship, and they and Michelle's mom are all happy together in the White House. And they recently hit a new milestone in their marriage: their twentieth wedding anniversary.

By taking personal responsibility for your own happiness and making space for your partner to be who and what he is, magic can and often does happen. The blame-shame game has no space to breathe when personal responsibility is in the room.

Put on Those Rose-Colored Glasses!

Although I would never suggest that we should go into denial when our partner is acting out or being difficult, there is research that now proves that there are strong benefits to wearing your rose-colored glasses when viewing your mate.

Dr. Sandra Murray, a psychologist at the University of Buffalo, has studied this phenomenon extensively and reveals that putting on the "rose-colored glasses" and idealizing our partner actually leads to more happiness and satisfaction in relationships.[10] In fact, the happiest couples focus on what's right and not on what's wrong. This is also known as the Pygmalion effect, the phenomenon in which the greater the expectation placed upon people, the better they perform. It's a form of self-fulfilling prophecy. As mature adults, we get to choose our thoughts and beliefs, so why not focus on the best in, actively intend the best for, and expect the best out of ourselves and our partners?

Here are the sad but true facts about marriage today: 50 percent of first marriages, 67 percent of second marriages, and 73 percent of third marriages end in divorce.[11] Modern-day society has conditioned us to look for and see perfection, which leads to an ongoing state of frustration and dissatisfaction. In truth, we all know that perfection is not possible. But by changing our story and practicing some Wabi Sabi Love, we can come to appreciate our own and our partner's imperfection and can actually experience a more natural state of grace than we thought possible.

Wabi Sabi Love and Sex

There is now ample research proving that pleasure not only reduces stress; it also improves our health, overall well-being, and longevity. This probably isn't surprising, but when was the last time you consciously added even simple pleasures to your life?

The Wabi Sabi approach to pleasure doesn't require much effort; rather, it consists of small, simple actions. Begin by making a list of things that evoke pleasure in each of your senses, and then promise yourself to take at least one pleasure break a day.

Here are a few of the ways I take quick solo pleasure breaks:

> I love the fragrance of scented candles as well as the warm, soft dancing of a flame, so I curl up in my favorite chair, light a candle, and indulge for a few minutes with a piece of my favorite chili chocolates.

> If I have had a particularly stressful day, I take a long warm bath, soaking in my aromatherapy oils, surrounded by candles and soft music.

If I want to pump up my energy, I put on a high-energy Latin-grooves CD of some of my favorite tunes, turn up the volume, and dance like crazy.

It's really quite simple. For the next week decide to take ten minutes each day to schedule a pleasure break just for you, even if it's just making a cup of your favorite tea or stopping to literally smell the roses.

Now, if you are married or in a long-term relationship, you might be surprised to discover that your grandparents had sex more often than you do. Our grandparents didn't have five hundred plus channels of television, Facebook, Twitter, and the Internet to distract them. It's very likely they had a lot more time for sex! We're a world of busy, overcommitted, stressed-out, sleep-deprived, and just plain tired folks.

For many couples, life just seems to get in the way of finding time for sexual pleasures. Frustration and dissatisfaction are not feelings conducive to an exciting sex life. To allow for more sex, more joy, and more harmony in our lives, it's time that we embrace Wabi Sabi in the bedroom too.

What if you made a date with your mate for a little Wabi Sabi sex? Applying Wabi Sabi to your sex life means it's okay that you're too tired, too stressed, or don't have time. You just decide to do it anyway, even if nobody really wants to.

According to relationship guru Alison Armstrong, just because you are not in the mood or feeling estranged or disconnected from your partner doesn't mean you can't make the effort to reconnect and reignite the energizing and life-giving forces of sex. It's like riding a bike—you'll quickly get back in the groove.

Here are a few ways to enhance your sexual experience:

- Be creative.

- Find a new time, a new place, a new way to initiate a connection.

- Even if you feel silly, awkward, or strange, just go for it.

- Remember this is Wabi Sabi sex—it doesn't have to be perfect.

And, however the lovemaking turns out, whether it's dull and routine or toe-curling ecstasy, choose to find the beauty and perfection in it. Know that it's going to be great, because you've made the effort to give yourself and your partner some attention, affection, and pleasure.

When we allow ourselves to experience pleasure, we are relaxed and in the flow and it's a zillion times easier to access our positive emotions. By taking the time to add pleasure to your life you will be calmer, happier, and more receptive to enjoying and receiving love at every level.

With Wabi Sabi Love you learn to accept the flaws, imperfections, and limitations—as well as the gifts and blessings—

that form your shared history as a couple. Acceptance and its counterpart, understanding, are crucial to achieving relationship harmony. It's sacred love, which is the highest form of love. As with most things worth striving for in life, it requires patience, commitment, personal responsibility, and practice. Imagine how great you will feel when you know your partner loves all of you, all the time—the good, the bad, and everything in between!

We have a lot more influence over our personal situation than we think. Whatever stories we choose to tell will inform the kind of relationship we will have with our mate. If we view our mate favorably, he or she will tend to live up to that truth. The same thing happens if we view our mate negatively. Gradually our mate will act out the very negative attributes we emphasize. As the saying goes, what we resist persists. Spewing negativity highlights what isn't working. Our attention goes to all the wrongdoings, which reinforces their impact. A shift in focus to what is working will create more trust, joy, and harmony. Either way, what we think and how we act upon those thoughts form our entire reality.

SEVEN

The Magic Power of Three

Divine love is without condition, without boundary, without change. The flux of the human heart is gone forever at the transfixing touch of pure love.

Sri Yukteswar

Whether you believe in a Higher Power or not, the fact is you two can't do this alone. Inviting a third party into your marriage in the form of Spirit will help you when your house is divided. It is always good to have a mediator as your guide, especially during those times when you have both hit the wall. The truth is, a powerful relationship stems from the magic of the triad of love: you, your mate, and God/Spirit/Universe.

Dr. Brian Weiss, America's leading authority on past-life regression therapy, claims: "If you look closely, you'll see that all the great religions are teaching about the same things: love, compassion, giving, nonviolence, and mindful awareness." I agree with Dr. Weiss. Even though I was raised Jewish, over the years I have studied and participated in many different spiritual traditions. These days I often refer to myself as a "spiritual mutt." I believe that there is an unseen force for good, universally available to all, that can be called into our lives through the power of prayer and awareness.

When I pray, it is not, "Dear God, please bring me X, Y, and Z." It is a prayer of gratitude, thanking God for "already having fulfilled my desire." For instance, if I am having an upset or break with someone, my prayer would be: "Dear God, thank you for showing me the way to heal my issues with _____. I am grateful that this problem has already been easily and effortlessly resolved for the highest good of all parties involved. And so it is."

Having some kind of relationship with a Higher Power can be especially useful when you are feeling lost, out of control, or helpless. As the Christian tradition states, wherever two or more are gathered, God enters the room. In my view, you can bring that power into your life by expressing gratitude every day. Even if your partner does not share your view, gratitude and love are universal energies with amazing healing properties. Inviting a spiritual aspect into your relationship can help you ride even the roughest waters more smoothly.

Inviting God into Your Love Life

One of the most important and life-changing books I've ever read is *Conversations with God,* by Neale Donald Walsch. When I read it more than twenty years ago, I was so profoundly moved by the powerful, transformational content that I picked up the phone, called information, found Neale's phone number, and called him!

When Neale answered, I thanked him profusely for writing the book. We spoke for quite a while, and he asked me what I did for a living. I explained that I was a book publicist, to which he replied: "We should work together." That was the start of a friendship spanning several decades.

In a 2013 interview for the Art of Love Relationship Series, I asked him how being in a love relationship helps us. Here's what he said:

> It creates a field that we can step into and grow to become and to experience, to declare and express, the grandest idea that we ever had about who we are. A relationship provides us with moment-to-moment, day-to-day opportunities to step into that, even when the people we love become challenging. It's the very challenge that relationship presents to us that is our grandest invitation from God. God is asking us, especially in our relationship life, a single question: "What aspect of me do you choose to demonstrate now?"

Wow. That really got me thinking. In every moment, how do I want to show up for my beloved? How can I become the grand-est version of myself in life and in love? Spending that time with Neale, I felt a shift within myself. I felt my heart open-ing and expanding to the point of really aspiring to become a grander version of myself on all levels.

One of the ways I have become a "grander version of my-self" revealed itself to me recently. My friend Carol Allen, of *Love Is in the Stars* fame, connected me with a new "love" expert and we had a nice long phone conversation about the book and products he has created to help people find more intimacy in their relationships. After our call, this man sent me an e-mail that opened with "I feel so loved by you!" Wow. That totally made my day.

For years I have observed Brian interact with everyone he comes in contact with from a place of love, care, consideration, and patience. I have secretly aspired to be more like him. Although it took many years for me to evolve into a person who interacts in a more loving way with strangers, I now had con-firmation that this "more loving Arielle" had emerged.

We can't always be the highest version of ourselves. It is hard to maintain that level of consciousness at all times, but having a clear intention is the first step. I also think it's useful to have our own definition of what divinity is for us. Whether you call the divinity God, Goddess, the Universe, the Force, the Higher Self, or whatever, striving to lift ourselves and those around us can only bring more good into our lives and to the world.

When well-respected spiritual teacher and author Panache Desai was interviewed by Oprah on her show *Super Soul Sunday,* Oprah asked him to define God. Panache sat in silence for a very long beat and then answered:

There isn't a definition for God. Any words that I would use to answer this question would diminish what God is.

God is not definable, but if I were to attempt to describe what God is, it would be along these lines: God is love, a force, and a vibration for all that is sacred, good, and holy. In my view, God exists as a divine ocean of love and mercy. We are all a part of God. Together we are all merged with the Universe to be an experience of God.

Because we are hardwired for love, our desire and drive for love serves as a conduit to feel closer to God. The desire for a mortal beloved is a physical manifestation of our sometimes forgotten connection to the divine. The roly-polies I described in Chapter 1 represent our togetherness as an expression of divinity incarnate.

Expressing our love for one another is an excellent way to have an experience of God, which is why it makes sense to consciously choose to invite God into our relationship. This invitation helps us move beyond our ordinary behavior to achieve a higher, more spiritual awareness of our union. By inviting and welcoming God into your relationship, you literally build in a safety net, a net that can catch you when you "forget" the innocence of your partner or yourself. The divine offers a safety net to fall into when your partner's humanness has pushed your buttons to the maximum and you are on the verge of giving up.

Neale Donald Walsch believes that by inviting God into our relationship, it broadens, enhances, and enlarges the relationship experience by bringing in the divine energy, or God energy:

> There is no place you can go and nothing you can do that God is not already a part of. When we imagine ourselves to be a spiritual being, to have a soul and to be a spiritual being that is traveling with a body and a mind through time and space, through eternity, and we see our romantic love partner to be the same, that will dramatically change the nature of the relationship and how we interact.

When I asked my dear friend the wise and wondrous Sadhvi Bhagawati Saraswati, who is a spiritual teacher in Rishikesh, India, how to invite God into a relationship, she explained it this way:

> God is already there. That which we deeply connect to within another person, that deep sense of Soul/Spirit *is* God. Think about it, Arielle. Every single cell of your being has changed since you've married Brian—as has every single cell of him—so who is loving whom? Where is the Arielle who loved Brian when you got married? That which is unchanging, eternal, nonphysical *is* God. So it's not so much the Elijah situation, where we have to remember to leave the cup out for him and prop the door open, but rather that when we interact with each other we have to truly realize that it's not just this body and that body; this history and

that history; this set of neuroses and that set of neuroses; you're a round peg for my round hole type of thing. That real love *is* about the merging of the self into the Self, which is with God. The relationship is just a medium. That's why when people ask about the best way to connect with God I always say it doesn't matter. Just connect. So if you're really melting in LOVE, not just the physiological rush of oxytocin and endorphins, but real LOVE, then you can be sure it's not just you and him, but you, him, God within you, God within him, and the infinite, boundless God everywhere.

The spiritual teacher, author, and lecturer Marianne Williamson explains it this way:

> When I look at another human being, and I want them to take away all of my existential pain and my sense of loneliness in the Universe, this is not helpful. This is dysfunctional because I'm looking to another human being to be in my life what only God can be. When I look at the other human being as my partner in finding God, my partner through the experience of unconditional love between us, and deep vulnerability, deep authenticity within us and total communication within us, that means that both of us are holding the space for God's presence in both of our lives and in the relationship. In this holy relationship we both end up revealing the wounds and scars of our childhood and through this process we begin to heal and understand that the purpose of this relationship is to heal spiritually, emotionally, and psychologically.[12]

In her book *Illuminata,* Marianne offers the following prayer for couples:

Dear God,

Please make of our relationship a great and holy adventure.

May our joining be a sacred space.

May the two of us find rest here, a haven for our souls.

Remove from us any temptation to judge one another or to direct one another.

We surrender to You our conflicts and our burdens.

We know You are our answer and our rock.

Help us to not forget.

Bring us together in heart and mind as well as body.

Remove from us the temptation to criticize or be cruel.

May we not be tempted by fantasies and projections,

But guide us in the ways of holiness.

Save us from darkness.

May this relationship be a burst of light.

May it be a fount of love and wisdom for us, for our family, for our community, for our world.

May this bond be a channel for Your love and healing, a vehicle of Your grace and power.

As lessons come and challenges grow, let us not be tempted to forsake each other.

Let us always remember that in each other we have the most beautiful woman, the most beautiful man,

The strongest one,

The sacred one in whose arms we are repaired.

May we remain young in this relationship.

Bring us what You desire for us,

And show us how You would have us be.

Thank You, dear God,

You who are the cement between us.

Thank You for this love.

Amen.[13]

My friend the Reverend Cynthia James teaches that spirituality is an awakening or a so-called remembrance. Because we are all connected to the Universe, she claims we are all emanations of spiritual energy, divine at the core of our being. When we are nurtured from and tap into that place for all of our decisions, we gain immense clarity, health, and well-being.

When she and her husband, Carl Studna, first connected, they were doing different spiritual practices, yet they shared the same commitment to their own growth. Most important, they believed that the best communication comes from the heart. Today, they share two daily spiritual practices. Each morning they meditate together and at night, before bed, they acknowledge themselves for the accomplishments of the day that made them proud. Finally, they take turns acknowledging and appreciating three things about each other.

Cynthia suggests that if your partner is not spiritual, it's important to find things to nurture your own soul and spiritual growth. Whether it's meditation, yoga, guided processes, or online classes, she encourages you to find communities, churches, or groups in order to be nurtured and grow spiritually.

Inviting God into your relationship as the defining factor in your personal trinity of love is to invite healing and the possibility for unconditional love. But what if you have a partner who doesn't share your belief in God?

When Gabrielle Bernstein first met her husband-to-be, Zach, he didn't necessarily subscribe to all of her beliefs. As one of America's up-and-coming spiritual leaders, Gabrielle was serious about the benefits of her practice, but not pushy or demanding that he join in. Instead, each morning, Gabrielle would say her prayers, read passages from books like *A Course in Miracles,* and trust that she and Zach would find a way to make a life together.

"I just live and walk my talk and invite spirit to do her thing. And as a result of witnessing my practice, my husband began to open to it," Gabrielle explains. Together they also created a very special ritual. Every morning before Zach walks out the door to go to work, Gabrielle places her hands on him in silent blessing—asking the angels to keep them both safe, happy, and healthy. Actively praying for and blessing your soulmate is a beautiful way to affirm your love.

There is a Hindu tradition in northern India that offers an elaborate and beautiful ritual to celebrate the sanctity of marriage. Known as the festival of Karwa Chauth, it occurs each year on the fourth day after the full moon during October or November. Married women spend an entire day praying and fasting for their husband as a way to show their love, devotion, and respect as well as to ensure the continued health, well-being, and prosperity of their beloved.

Preparation for the event begins days earlier. Traditionally, the women dress up as brides and often buy new clothes and jewelry to look their best. Like brides, many also apply the traditional henna to their hands and feet.

On the day of Karwa Chauth, they rise before dawn and eat fruit or dried fruit provided by their mothers-in-law. The fasting begins at sunrise and lasts until they see the moon in the sky. Once they see the moon, they gather with other women to "break the fast" while making offerings of plates of fruits and sweets to the moon.

Historically this ritual has been for women, who fast for their husbands, but today more and more Indian men are joining their wives and fasting, because they have come to understand that they need their wives as much as the wives need them.

The Salmon, the Fisherman, and the King

My sister, Debbie, loved her rabbi, Baruch Ezagui, particularly for his deep wisdom and very special storytelling prowess. When I shared with him that I was writing this book, he surprised me by explaining that the Jewish tradition doesn't really believe in soulmates. "The Torah," he says, "implies that your soulmate is your soul, not a partner. The Torah looks at the other gender as opposition to you to find a whole new way of defining your existence . . . to push you into a place you have never been before." Then he shared this story.

A fisherman is fishing on a lake in the middle of nowhere. He feels a tug on his line and sees a most magnificent salmon. As he is reeling in the salmon, he knows not only that this is the most beautiful salmon he has ever seen, but that the king loves salmon, and if he brings it to him, it will make him a national hero. The fisherman puts the prized salmon into a bucket of water and heads to shore.

While hanging out in the bucket, the salmon thinks to himself, "At least I am still alive; maybe there is hope for me."

When the fisherman arrives at the castle, the guards at the gate take one look at the salmon and agree that the king will be thrilled to have it. The fisherman is then brought to the throne room, where everyone gathers over the bucket and agrees that this is the most amazing salmon ever.

The king looks into the bucket and says, "This is beyond my wildest dreams. I have never seen such a salmon in all my life."

The salmon, knowing he has been praised by the king, now thinks to himself, "I am going to live like a prince! The king is going to take care of me."

Then the king proclaims, "This salmon is so beautiful, I am going to eat it for my dinner. Take it immediately to the chef for tonight's state dinner."

The salmon is now deeply depressed upon hearing his impending fate.

As the chef begins to slice the salmon, the salmon speaks to the chef: "My friend, the king does not love salmon. If he did, I would still be swimming in the ocean!"

Rabbi Ezagui explains the meaning of this story:

True love is loving the person for what they love, who they are, for what they stand for. If you go into a marriage loving what you love, not what *they* love, that is not love. Real love is not finding someone to hold your hand and find common ground with; the institution of marriage is to push you out of your comfort zone, to lift you up above what you *need,* so that you can provide *what you're needed for.*

According to Rabbi Ezagui, marriage is the highest calling of humankind. "It includes the marriage between body and soul, heaven and earth, spirit and matter, one human and another. This union of beings is reflected in the marriage between men and women."

Marriage is about finding out what we truly need. It also fulfills our need to be needed. Rabbi Ezagui quotes Rebbe Lubavitch, who said: "When you learn to love someone else as you love yourself, when you get to that level and you can truly authentically say that other person is me [at a soul level], that is the purpose of life." Rabbi Ezagui's mentor Rabbi Mendel Futerfas claims that as long as the man treats his wife like a queen, he will be a king, an attitude that should be ingrained long before the wedding and carried on long after the reality of life kicks in. People with strong marriages consider this idea as nonnegotiable.

Rabbi Ezagui says:

> The concept of prayer itself is the preparation for marriage. It's not that I stand with my hands out asking for mercy or God's kindness. In Judaism prayer is the way to connect as an opportunity to put yourself on the same wavelength as the blessing. The answer is already there. It's just "Dear God period." It is about acknowledging that everything and every moment is a reflection of God's inner existence, the moment I recognize that I don't need anything. God doesn't need. I don't need. What is required is to find in my soul *what I am needed for*.

My friend Inga recently experienced this in her life. She is married to Jack Canfield, bestselling author and cocreator of the Chicken Soup for the Soul series. Jack is easily one of the most generous men I have ever met. A true giver, Jack works incredibly hard writing, teaching, traveling, coaching, and mentoring. From Inga's perspective Jack is married to thousands of people around the world. Most nights, by the time he comes home, he has given and given to all the people in his life, and for the past several years Inga has often thought, "There is nothing left for him to give to me."

> The soul is your innermost being. The presence that you are beyond form. The consciousness that you are beyond form, that is the soul. That is who you are in essence.
>
> *Eckhart Tolle*

Inga and Jack recently went through a bumpy time in their marriage, where she felt as if she was simply Jack's "refueling station." Inga began to really question whether the marriage was over, and the thought terrified her. She was overwhelmed with their busy life and how much it takes from them. She couldn't and didn't know how to move forward with him. In her head she was thinking, "It's over," because that is what happened in her childhood home.

As she searched her heart for answers, Inga came to realize that she had been afraid to share with Jack her deepest feelings for him. She saw that she hadn't stood up and fought for their love, and she hadn't taken a stand for their marriage. She hadn't admitted to herself, or to him, just how much she really *did* want to make it work.

Gathering up her courage, Inga finally woke Jack up in the middle of the night to tell him how much she loved him. She opened her heart and shared with him how much she wanted to spend the rest of her life with him. Jack's immediate loving and enthusiastic response was all the affirmation she needed to be reminded of how much he really does love her.

Today Inga has transformed her thinking and now says, "I'm Jack's wife, and the greatest gift I can give him is to choose, every day, to fill up his tank." By consciously choosing to be Jack's "refueling station," she not only fills him up, thus helping to fill the world, she also fills herself up with love and joy.

There is an old saying that it takes two to tango, but as Rabbi Ezagui says, "Life is not a tango. Life is ultimately graduating from the tango, graduating from the struggle, and finding the simplicity of truth and absoluteness of what is, as it is."

There are two very powerful words in the English language: "Why me?" According to Rabbi Ezagui, the phrase can either be an eternal question or a question with a possible answer. One implies reaction, the other action. If, instead of the reactive "Why me?" you can ask yourself, "Why (is there a) me? What am I here for?" the reactive question will disappear. Loving *what is* takes courage, patience, and a lot of understanding. When you reach this level of grace, the struggle ends.

The Centering Nature of God

Thirty-five years ago a divine conspiracy brought together two deeply spiritual people, both of whom were ready to spend their lives alone unless they found a partner who was committed to a relationship in which God came first. By the second week of dating, Jerry Jampolsky, author of the bestselling book *Love Is Letting Go of Fear,* and Diane Cirincione, a psychologist, discovered their mutual passion to lead a life in which God would come before anything else.

As Jerry explains, "The only real relationship is with God. Neither of us knew if we would ever find a partner who thought like that."

"And when we did," says Diane, "it became the pivotal point in our relationship. By inviting God into our relationship, we invite every being that we come into contact with as a part of God. Our challenge and our choice is to see the Higher Self in everyone."

Jerry adds, "It means that we live in the present, not the past or the future, being compassionate, knowing that our relationship with everyone is a *joining,* not a *separation.* We look at people as if through the eyes of God."

Diane concludes, "Another way we experience this is to act and be as if there is a presence in the room . . . because there is. There is not a God who judges; there is only love."

Every day before calls and meetings Jerry and Diane pray together, reciting a prayer they adapted from the original version in *A Course in Miracles:*

> We are here only to be truly helpful.
> We are here to represent You who sent us.

We don't have to worry about what to say or what to do.
Because You who sent us will direct us.
We are content to be wherever You wish,
Knowing that You are always going there with us
And we will be healed as we let you teach us to heal.
Amen.[14]

At the end they then add the following line onto the original form of the prayer:

Let us step aside and let You lead the way.

Prayer is helpful to keep you centered in times of distress or discomfort as well. Jerry has also been known to pray for guidance when he makes a rare outing to the mall with Diane.

Shop, Pray, Love

Like many men I know, Jerry used to hate shopping, and luckily for him his beloved wife, Diane, doesn't go shopping very often. However, on those rare occasions when she does hit the mall, she likes to have Jerry come along. From the start, Jerry would glance at his watch frequently, making it obvious that he would rather not be there; in turn, Diane often felt pressured to rush through what used to be an enjoyable pastime.

One afternoon, as Jerry was anxiously biding his time while he sat in the middle of the dress department, he closed his eyes and literally asked God for help in dealing with what felt to him like an unbearable situation. Almost instantaneously, he received very clear and specific instructions: instead of waiting impatiently for their shopping expedition to end, he was to take out his pen and write Diane a love poem. Jerry followed this spiritual prompting, and as he did, he was overcome with a great sense of peace. Not only was he reconnecting with his love for Diane, but he had also made the shift from focusing on only his own preferences to a state of gratitude for the life they shared together. Rather than being bored and antsy, he became engaged and enlivened by discovering a different way to relate to the process of shopping altogether.

In the middle of this transformation, Diane came to show him a dress she wanted to buy and found Jerry sitting peacefully with a smile on his face. Confused but intent on shopping, she went back to trying on more clothes. After a brief interlude, she came back to check on him again. He was still calm and peaceful. After she had made her purchases, she went to find him so they could finally leave before the experience inflicted any further damage. He asked her to sit down and said, "I'd like to share something with you."

Jerry quietly read her the beautiful love poem he had written as a tribute to her. She thanked him as her eyes filled with tears and the shutters on her heart blew wide open. They left the store giggling and holding hands in a bubble of love no shopping high could match. To this day, whenever they find themselves at a mall, Jerry writes her love poems.

But the story continues. Jerry's "message from God" moment not only helped him and his wife; his epiphany helped a total stranger too. One day Diane was in a department store, shopping with her mother. She saw a young woman quickly going through the clothing racks while a young man sitting nearby was looking miserable. Diane approached the man with a smile.

"It's really horrible, isn't it?" she softly said to him.

"Yes," he said, dipping his head down as if not wanting to admit the torture he felt. "I really hate this."

"My husband used to feel this way too," Diane said. She surveyed the young man's face for a moment.

"Used to?" he asked, sitting up a little straighter.

Diane shared her story about how much Jerry hated shopping until God suggested he begin using the time to write her exquisite love poems.

The young man listened intently without saying a word. For a moment, he paused with a look of uncertainty on his face. Just as Diane drew back, hoping she hadn't overstepped her bounds, the young man leaped from his seat and called out to his wife who was closing in on the dressing room with an armful of clothes.

"Um, honey, do you have a pen?"

EIGHT

Wild Abandon

Your Brain on Love

If you live to a hundred,
I want to live to be a hundred minus one day,
so I never have to live without you.

Winnie the Pooh

Our eyes lock across a crowded room and suddenly we have butterflies in our stomach. We meet, our hands touch, the mating dance begins, and we can barely think of anything or anyone else. Our brain and bloodstream fill with a chemical cocktail that includes neurotrophin, a nerve growth factor, and we are officially lovestruck. Our brain's pleasure center is fully activated for six months and up to two years, what's called the "honeymoon phase," and then it all slowly disappears.

Feelings of romantic love are both pleasurable and physically stressful. It is literally a chemical high, often compared to the feelings you get after a snort of cocaine.

The process of falling in love, also known as limerence, is a necessary step to long-term love. Some consider it the short-term superglue that brings couples together initially, so that they will eventually bond for a long-term relationship. Both limerence and love occur in the part of the brain called the insula, which assigns value and which is also the part of the brain affected by addiction. The difference between healthy love and addiction is quite clear. Healthy love is not an addiction; it is a joyful life-affirming state of being. Addiction comes with obsessive and negative behaviors.

When you fall in love, your brain literally goes haywire.[15] Neurons transmit messages down the slippery slides called synapses, which move the feel-good chemicals to the reward center of the brain, called the caudate nucleus, and the neighboring ventral tegmental area. Your brain is on a dopamine high as you gaze lovingly at your seemingly infallible partner. You block out any thoughts of annoyance or possible fault in the other person. You are actually blinded by your brain . . . and your heart.

It is no wonder we feel crazy for a while. The truth is the body can't sustain that kind of activity forever. After about two years, the neurotransmitters stop sending messages to the reward center in our heads, and a new kind of love sets in.

Naturally, a new kind of love requires a different type of hormone. That's where oxytocin, also known as the bonding hormone or "nature's love glue," comes in. High oxytocin levels are correlated with the success of long-term relationships. The more oxytocin you have, the more your body makes, which positively impacts your relationship.

Scientific research proves there is indeed a relationship between love and brain chemistry. Based on that knowledge, I am going to show you how to kick-start your way back to love and connection.

Ignite Your Love Through More Pleasure Points

Even though your brain has calmed down after the initial rush of falling in love, it does not mean you can't experience the pleasures that long-lasting love can offer. I am a firm believer that there is always room in life for more love and more pleasure. Activating or creating more loving and pleasurable feelings is something we can take steps to do. Here's how.

When you want to feel more love, you can consciously do things that actively release the hormone oxytocin into your brain. Oxytocin is really good for you, and according to love master Dr. John Gray women need to constantly rebuild their oxytocin levels. Taking time for a nice manicure, getting your hair done, enjoying a massage, taking a long warm bubble bath, listening to music, dancing, walking in nature, quietly sipping a cup of tea, and savoring a perfect piece of chocolate or your favorite treat are a few ways to add pleasure to your daily life that also *rebuild oxytocin.*

Stress is one of the main reasons oxytocin becomes depleted, so taking simple steps to rebuild it is necessary to maintain a happy, healthy lifestyle. Oxytocin can be generated lots of ways, and the more you have, the better you will feel. Not surprisingly, it plays a big role in producing orgasms.

By taking the time to add pleasure to your life, you will be calmer, happier, and more receptive to enjoying and attracting love at every level. It's well known that a simple twenty-second hug, gazing into the eyes of someone you care about, or petting your dog or cat will also boost your oxytocin level. Going shopping also does the trick. Even if you don't buy anything, just looking at and touching beautiful items makes a difference.

Other oxytocin-inducing activities include:

- Going to a live outdoor concert and soaking in the music through every sense

- Slowly eating and savoring your favorite dessert

- Laughing

- Lighting candles and taking a nice long bubble bath

- Dancing

- Having a good gab with a girlfriend

- Doing something silly like playing charades with a group of friends

- Saying "I love you" to someone

- Singing karaoke

- Watching a tear-jerker movie

There is a tremendous amount of new research that proves the importance of having pleasure in our lives. When we are relaxed and in the flow, it's a zillion times easier to access and emit our positive emotions.

Another benefit of high oxytocin levels is they help in keeping your weight down. Researchers have observed that mice deficient in oxytocin or oxytocin receptors become obese later in life, even with normal food intake. Scientists who have given oxytocin-deficient obese mice oxytocin infusions saw their weight return to normal levels. The mice also showed a reduced glucose intolerance and insulin resistance. This clearly suggests an alternative option for those struggling to keep the weight off.

My personal "pleasure recipe" includes a daily bath with aromatherapy, an early morning walk with my husband, and one-on-one time with my cat Yoda. If I have a particularly stressful day, I have a special CD of favorite dance tunes that I crank up in my office. I dance and sing along all by myself until I feel the endorphins surging through me.

If consciously adding pleasure to your daily life doesn't come naturally to you, I would suggest a little experiment. For the next seven days, decide to add at least fifteen to twenty minutes of pleasure a day *all for you*. As you create your to-do list, put yourself at the top of that list. Remember, what you put your attention on grows.

As you can see, hormones can be helpful in putting yourself in the right head and heart space for greater happiness. By increasing your oxytocin levels, you will have more love for yourself and more love to share with your soulmate, family, and friends.

In addition to the fact that oxytocin creates a yummy environment in your brain for more love, it turns out that when you fall in love with someone, your brain circuitry becomes "hardwired" to love this person, even when you experience difficult times with him or her. Even if it's just the stress of day-to-day existence with your partner or you break up, move away, and don't see the person for decades, it's possible to "reignite" the love. This brain circuitry is like a sleeping cat and can be awakened at any time.

Before we look at how to "wake up that sleeping cat," it's useful to understand a bit more about your brain and love. In her book *Why We Love: The Nature and Chemistry of Romantic Love,* Dr. Helen Fisher, anthropologist, love expert, Rutgers University professor, and the most referenced scholar in the love research community, says: "My research has proven to me that everywhere, people fall into romantic love. I have come to see this passion as a fundamental human drive. Like the craving for food and water and the maternal instinct, it is a psychological need, a profound urge, an instinct to court and win a particular mating partner."

Anthropologists have found evidence for romantic love in 177 societies around the world. It's nearly universal that people will sing for love, dance for love, pine for love, and yes, even die for love!

From her decades of research Fisher believes that humanity has evolved three core brain systems responsible for directing love, mating, and reproduction. These manifest as:

> Lust: the sex drive or libido, including the craving for sexual satisfaction (testosterone)
>
> Romantic love and attraction: the early stage of intense romantic love (dopamine)
>
> Attachment: the deep feelings of peace, security, and union with a long-term partner (oxytocin)

Love can start off with any of these three feelings, lust, attraction, or attachment, Fisher maintains. Each of the three systems is triggered by chemicals evolved to serve a different function. Together they enable mating, pair bonding, and parenting:

1. Our sex drive evolved to encourage us to seek a range of partners in order for the human species to propagate.

2. Later, romantic love, a refinement of mere lust, evolved to enable us to focus our energy on just one potential mate. Characterized by feelings of exhilaration and intrusive, obsessive thoughts about the object of one's affection, this mental state may share neurochemical

characteristics with the manic phase of bipolar disorder. Dr. Fisher suggests that the actual behavioral patterns of those in love, such as attempting to evoke reciprocal responses in one's loved one, can even resemble obsessive-compulsive disorder. All of the dopamine flooding your system is what causes the butterflies in your stomach and pumps up feelings of euphoria.

3. Given that romantic love is not sufficiently stable and anchoring for long-term cooperative child rearing, attachment evolved to enable us to feel deeply connected to our partner long enough to accomplish this. This state, according to Fisher, is characterized by feelings of calm, security, social comfort, and emotional union. Years later when lovebirds become less obsessive and more bonded, things begin to feel less exciting, as brain chemistry begins to normalize. As less dopamine is released, it doesn't mean the bond is dying, but rather that a molecule called corticotropin-releasing factor (CRF) is released, which helps keep couples together. In fact, when you and your beloved are separated, CRF is the cause of "missing each other." Also, for men, vasopressin increases. In healthy relationships this is what makes us remain loyal and protective of our partners. It literally promotes fidelity!

Quite simply, we are wired for romance, love, and attachment. The brain chemistry cocktail that leads to love, even if it has fizzled out and fallen flat, can be intentionally "shaken and stirred" to awaken the "sleeping cat," if you will. Fisher offers many suggestions to reignite the chemistry, including the most obvious one: have more sex with your partner, even if you are both so busy that you need to "make appointments for sex."

"When you make love with someone, you drive up the testosterone system, which makes you want more sex," explains Fisher. "Any stimulation of the genitals drives up the dopamine system and creates and sustains feelings of romantic love. With orgasm, your brain floods with oxytocin and vasopressin. Both are linked with feelings of attachment." Not only is sex good for you and your relationship, seminal fluid has a lot of great chemicals for women, including some that reduce depression!

To retrigger feelings of love, Fisher suggests doing novel things together. When you do something challenging together, it causes arousal and drives up dopamine. Whether it's taking a vacation to a new city or country or learning to dance, doing new things together outside of your comfort zone gives you feelings of romantic love. This is why taking a vacation often becomes a sexy adventure.

Fisher believes that in order to trigger attachment, we need to "literally" stay in touch. "Learn to start out sleeping in each other's arms at night. Walk arm in arm. Hold hands, kiss, play footsie under the table at dinner, massage each other. Touch drives up the oxytocin system," says Fisher.

She also recommends a practice of saying five nice things to your partner every day: "It's good for them and it's great for your immune system, blood pressure, and your heart."

How do you know if you are still in love with your mate? Dr. Fisher and her research partner, Dr. Lucy L. Brown, offer a fantastic quiz where you can discover if you really are "in love." They call it the Love Calculator, and it measures the Passionate Love Scale. You can take the quiz for free at www .theanatomyoflove.com.

Another form of novelty is to actually seek out circumstances that will trigger fear. Bear with me now. It really works! By leveraging your fear and the resulting brain chemistry stemming from it, you can create a stronger bond with your partner.

The Bonding Nature of Fear

A few years ago I was watching a dating show on television in which a couple on their second date decided to bungee jump from a bridge. It was something neither of them had ever done before. Not only were they going to leap off the bridge; they were also going to do it at the same time.

First, they sat on the edge of the bridge, side by side, admitting how scared they were. Then, as it was nearing time for the jump, they tried to crack a few jokes to distract themselves. You could tell they were petrified. At last they mustered the courage to jump. And guess what? They survived. In the next scene they were having a glass of wine, gazing into each other's eyes, and clearly falling in love.

How did that happen? One minute they were scared out of their wits and the next they were wining and dining one another in a state of pure bliss. What the TV viewers witnessed was the power of adrenaline and a dash of cortisol, the so-called stress hormone.

According to some experts, it just so happens that the physiological experience of fear and anxiety can lead to sexual attraction and bonding. If you are ready to "restart the love engines" with your mate and "up" the connection, it may be time to do something that includes enough risk to get the juices flowing again. Like recharging a dead car battery, it is a short-term solution, but it may be just the thing to get the ball rolling in the direction you want it to go.

Have you considered skydiving, whitewater rafting, riding a roller coaster, parasailing, or watching a really scary movie? You get the idea. Extreme emotions bring people together. They have the power of stripping away the nonsense to help you clearly see the reality of the situation. By placing yourself in a situation in which it feels as if there is the danger of death, you are also bringing yourselves closer together.

On a side note, some psychologists call this kind of situation "misattribution." It means to mistake the origin of your feelings toward another person, typically after being under dire circumstances together.[16] It is comparable to the behavior "drunk texting," in which a person sends a love message to another under the influence of alcohol and then quickly regrets it. It is typical in superficial relationships that don't last long.

Here's a good example of misattribution. In 1994 supermodel Christie Brinkley was in the process of divorcing singer Billy Joel, when she began dating real-estate developer Rick Taubman. They decided to go heli-skiing and nearly died when the helicopter crashed. The intensity of the experience brought them closer together, so they soon married and had one son. They divorced eleven months later.

Chances are you have been with your partner for some time, so most likely this phenomenon does not apply to you. Nonetheless it is good to recognize the short-term effect of extreme experiences on human behavior. This approach is about jump-starting your passion, not sustaining it. Other work must be done to lay the groundwork for a lasting relationship.

If your relationship has been traumatized by betrayal or some other deep wounding, it is still possible to reignite the love. In such cases, it is always wise to seek professional couples counseling to guide you through the healing process of rebuilding trust and respect. A third party can often maintain the neutral ground you need, while you both navigate a way back to each other through the hurt.

Generating Intimacy and Kick-Starting Love

Another very positive way to kick-start your love is to look at ways to increase your level of intimacy. Intimacy is the foundation for a solid, long-lasting relationship. It is the cornerstone of love.

In an intimacy study headed by State University of New York psychology professor Arthur Aron, a team of researchers discovered a method for creating closeness between two strangers. In a laboratory setting, the team asked participants to use a catalog of thirty-six increasingly personal questions and to then perform an exercise of silently looking into each other's eyes for four minutes.[17] The idea was to have participants discover three common traits and engage in a series of other trust-building measures to quickly create trust and intimacy, the cornerstones of any lasting relationship.

In an article in the *New York Times*, University of British Columbia writing instructor Mandy Len Catron recounts her experience of reenacting the experiment with a university colleague.[18] The intensity of the exercise was overwhelming. After several hours of conversation with her male colleague, she revealed that love is indeed an action. To their surprise, the test worked, and they fell in love.

Below are the thirty-six questions that Aron and his team originally put together to create closeness between two strangers. Did it work? These deep and probing questions have broken down emotional barriers between thousands of strangers, resulting in friendships, romance, and even some marriages. It turns out that answering these questions can also bring you and your partner closer together!

Carissa Ray, a supervising multimedia producer at Today .com who did this exercise with her partner of twelve years, discovered that their relationship has stood the test of time beyond the notion of romantic love. In an article, she says, "While we may not spend too many nights standing in the open air and staring into each other's 'windows of the soul,' we have spent many days and years speaking to each other with those same eyes, often without saying a word." She claims their answers show how they have defined each other's lives. "We don't have to pretend to be singles forcing our oral histories on one another after happy hour. We are family."[19]

When I had a chance to speak with her, she said the quiz reinforces the positive message: "You are my mate. I have chosen you." She recommends that couples take the time to reconnect.

The exercise takes about ninety minutes, but if you prefer to ask the questions over a longer period of time, that's okay too. The questions become increasingly more probing, so it is best to ask them in consecutive order. The main point of the exercise is for both you and your partner to start opening up to each other in ways you may not have for a long time.

INTIMACY EXERCISE

Set I

1. Given the choice of anyone in the world, whom would you want as a dinner guest?

2. Would you like to be famous? In what way?

3. Before making a telephone call, do you ever rehearse what you are going to say? Why?

4. What would constitute a "perfect" day for you?

5. When did you last sing to yourself? To someone else?

6. If you were able to live to the age of 90 and retain either the mind or body of a 30-year-old for the last 60 years of your life, which would you want?

7. Do you have a secret hunch about how you will die?

8. Name three things you and your partner appear to have in common.

9. For what in your life do you feel most grateful?

10. If you could change anything about the way you were raised, what would it be?

11. Take four minutes and tell your partner your life story in as much detail as possible.

12. If you could wake up tomorrow having gained any one quality or ability, what would it be?

Set II

13. If a crystal ball could tell you the truth about yourself, your life, the future, or anything else, what would you want to know?

14. Is there something that you've dreamed of doing for a long time? Why haven't you done it?

15. What is the greatest accomplishment of your life?

16. What do you value most in a friendship?

17. What is your most treasured memory?

18. What is your most terrible memory?

19. If you knew that in one year you would die suddenly, would you change anything about the way you are now living? Why?

20. What does friendship mean to you?

21. What roles do love and affection play in your life?

22. Alternate sharing something you consider a positive characteristic of your partner. Share a total of five items.

23. How close and warm is your family? Do you feel your childhood was happier than most other people's?

24. How do you feel about your relationship with your mother?

Set III

25. Make three true "we" statements each. For instance, "We are both in this room feeling . . ."

26. Complete this sentence: "I wish I had someone with whom I could share . . ."

27. If you were going to become a close friend with your partner, please share what would be important for him or her to know.

28. Tell your partner what you like about them; be very honest this time, saying things that you might not say to someone you've just met.

29. Share with your partner an embarrassing moment in your life.

30. When did you last cry in front of another person? By yourself?

31. Tell your partner something that you like about them already.

32. What, if anything, is too serious to be joked about?

33. If you were to die this evening with no opportunity to communicate with anyone, what would you most regret not having told someone? Why haven't you told them yet?

34. Your house, containing everything you own, catches fire. After saving your loved ones and pets, you have time to safely make a final dash to save any one item. What would it be? Why?

35. Of all the people in your family, whose death would you find most disturbing? Why?

36. Share a personal problem and ask your partner's advice on how he or she might handle it. Also, ask your partner to reflect back to you how you seem to be feeling about the problem you have chosen.

Once you and your partner have answered all thirty-six of these deep and penetrating questions, the final part of the exercise is this: stand or sit across from each other and lightly gaze into each other's eyes for four minutes in silence. Yes, it will likely feel uncomfortable and awkward, but do it anyway. This exercise, known as "eye gazing," is designed to connect you soul to soul and will help solidify the new bonds you have just created with each other.

As mentioned earlier, Mandy Len Catron sat down at a bar one night with a guy friend when they decided to answer the questions in Arthur Aron's study. They took several hours to answer all thirty-six questions and then did the final four minutes of eye gazing while standing on a bridge late at night. The two of them ultimately fell in love. In her article, she sums up her experience this way:

> The soul is the birthless, deathless, changeless part of us. The part of us that looks out beyond our eyes. The soul is infinite.
>
> *Wayne Dyer*

What I like about this study is how it assumes that love is an action. . . . Arthur Aron's study taught me that it's possible—simple, even—to generate trust and intimacy, the feelings love needs to thrive. . . . Although it's hard to credit the study entirely [for their falling in love] (it may have happened anyway), the study did give us a way into a relationship that feels deliberate. We spent weeks in the intimate space we created that night, waiting to see what it could become. Love didn't happen to us. We're in love because we each made the choice to be.

Like all things worth doing, kick-starting your love requires an investment of time, energy, intention, attention, and a real willingness to make it happen. The question then becomes "Are you committed enough to your relationship to go all in?" For most people, falling in love isn't hard, but choosing to stay in love requires commitment.

Although there will always be a myriad of definitions of love, one thing I know for sure is that love is based on a choice we make. Psychologist Erich Fromm says it beautifully: "Love is a decision. It is a judgment. It is a promise. If love were only a feeling, there would be no basis for the promise to love each other forever. A feeling comes and it may go. How can I judge that it will stay forever, when my act does not involve judgment and decision."

Making the decision, every day, sometimes even minute by minute, is the work of mature adults. We can't wait and hope to rely on "feeling love"; rather, we need to actively be "generating love" through our words, deeds, actions, and intentions. Especially in the moments when we really don't want to!

NINE

The Healing Power of Love

*To describe love is very difficult for the same
reason that words cannot fully describe the
flavor of an orange. You have to taste the fruit
to know its flavor. So with love.*

Paramahansa Yogananda

One night a few years ago, just after dinner, my beloved, Brian, sat me down on the couch and said something that was the equivalent of the heart-stopping phrase, "We have to talk." I remember experiencing this sinking feeling in the pit of my stomach, followed by the thought: "Oh no, what have I done?"

It was not long after the passing of my sister, Debbie, and we had both been through several brutal months, trying our best to survive as she slipped away from us. Neither one of us was getting much sleep, both of us were deep in our grief, and I was finally back at work trying to tackle not one, but three gigantic projects.

In the sweetest, most gentle voice, Brian began to share with me his massive concern for my health and well-being. With tears in his eyes, he told me he was afraid that, if I didn't stop the long, intense hours and stressing out so much, I would get very sick and possibly even "work myself to death."

As someone who has always been able to accomplish major things, juggle lots of simultaneous projects, and withstand huge amounts of pressure, I normally would have just assured him that I could "power" through this period and deal with it all. But there was something in the way he was approaching the conversation that made me stop and listen. His sincere, open-hearted vulnerability got through to me, and I really, really heard him.

And I saw that he was right. I was no longer the person who could do it all. My nervous system was shredded. I was out of "reserves" and running on fumes.

As I sat there, trying to take it all in, trying to figure out what to "do" about my situation, I remembered something Debbie whispered to me in the middle of the night: "Take more vacations."

I spent the next several days looking at the calendar, trying to see when I could take a vacation and for how long. And then it dawned on me. I didn't just need a week or two on a tropical island. I needed a big, long extended break. I needed to rest, rejuvenate, reboot, and rethink the rest of my life.

A few months later I stopped working—completely! I turned off my cell phone and put it in a drawer. I turned on the auto-responder on my e-mail and recorded a new voicemail on my phones to announce that for the next six weeks I would be completely, totally unavailable. I began my sabbatical.

I wondered: What if I get bored? How would I fill my days? Could I really do this? Completely unplug?

I am happy to report that it was a true success.

I began sleeping in, taking naps for the first time in my life, and reading all those books that had been languishing on my shelf. Brian and I played tennis and took tons of beach walks. We traveled to Bora Bora, Italy, and Romania. I began cooking more and resting a lot.

Every time I got an idea for a new project, I sat down, closed my eyes, took a deep breath, and waited for it to pass. If the idea persisted, I wrote it down and then forgot about it for the moment. I worked with my doctors to restore my energy levels and had many visits with the acupuncturist and chiropractor. My amazing partners at Evolving Wisdom gave me the huge gift of many massages.

During this healing time I decided to reinvent how I "do" life. One of my biggest aha moments was my new mantra: "I am now experiencing a new kind of aliveness that is not fueled by adrenaline."

Without the tyranny of a to-do list eating up every minute of my day, I made time to have some deep, meaningful conversations with several girlfriends who I've discovered are also "hitting the wall" and ready to make major changes. We have all admitted to being "busyness addicts," and we may even start a support group.

In the past I often defined myself by my work, and I hate to admit this, but my ego took a lot of pride in just how much I could accomplish in an hour or a day or a week. Years ago, when I worked as Deepak Chopra's publicist, he used to call me "speedy," and I thought that was a good thing! Too bad I wasn't listening more closely when Deepak was telling me how stressing out causes jittery platelets, which is not good for your health.

I then decided that I am done working for a living. I eliminated the word "work" from my vocabulary, and I now spend half my time diving into projects that provide me creative outlet, fun, and freedom and offer some level of contribution and prosperity.

Today my life has been radically transformed, because my loving and brave husband was willing to have a deep, life-changing conversation with me. There are many possible ways the conversation could have gone. He could have simply pointed his finger at me and said, "If you don't slow down, you're going to end up really hurting yourself," or something to that effect.

Instead, he really opened himself up, became "heart vulnerable," and allowed me to see the depth of his care and concern. The tears in his eyes, the look on his face, the compassion in his voice spoke to me in a way no accusation ever could. One of my patterns is to get defensive when accused of something, even if it's about something as important as my own well-being. Knowing that, Brian took a big risk in raising a sensitive topic. Because of his "heart vulnerability," I was able to really hear him, feel him, and commit to making life-saving changes.

"Being heart vulnerable is staying solidly centered in your heart, while you feel what's really going on. It's listening to your commonsense intelligence. It's not about being sentimental or mushy or letting others walk on you or allow their feelings to pull you down," explains Deborah Rozman, president and co-CEO of Quantum Intech, Inc., the parent company of HeartMath LLC.

"Being vulnerable doesn't have to be threatening, but it does take courage to be sincere, open, and honest. Often people avoid the feeling of vulnerability, because they are afraid of being pulled down into an emotional sinkhole they won't easily get out of," says Rozman.

Although some of us may perceive vulnerability as "wearing our hearts on our sleeves" or "letting it all spill out," it's really about loving with our whole heart, practicing gratitude, and leaning into joy, even in moments of terror. It is also about believing that you are "enough" and allowing yourself to be really seen.

Vulnerability means "sharing our feelings and our experiences with people who have earned the right to hear them," explains Brené Brown. Brown encourages us to take off our masks, to have the courage to be imperfect, the strength to love ourselves first, and the guts to let go of who we think we should be to become who we really are. She believes that vulnerability is at the core of fear, anxiety, and shame, but it is also the birthplace of joy, love, belonging, creativity, and faith.

In her TED talk "The Price of Invulnerability," Brown explains that as a culture we are losing our tolerance for vulnerability and that we have made vulnerability synonymous with weakness. "We live in a culture that tells us there is never enough: we are not enough. We are not good, safe enough, certain enough, perfect enough, not extraordinary enough. And yet, what's true is that in the ordinary moments of our life is where we can find the most joy," she says. On top of all of that, Brown claims that we "numb out" to avoid feeling vulnerable, and we do this by overeating, overspending, or staying too busy. The result is our inability to feel joy. We are numbed to the core.[20]

How many times have you opted to numb yourself in times of distress instead of looking the source of your pain square in the eye? We have all been there. The good news is there is a simple solution to not looking away, but rather welcoming it in through vulnerability. In order to embrace vulnerability, Brown suggests practicing gratitude.

"We stop and become thankful for what we have. We honor what's ordinary about our lives, that is what is truly extraordinary . . . the people we love, our family, being able to play, our community and nature. . . . In vulnerability we find what really gives purpose and meaning to our lives," says Brown.

According to medical doctor and author Mark Sircus, the most important key to love is found in our willingness and ability to be vulnerable. He explains that when we reach a level of true vulnerability, the heart opens up in an unobstructed fashion. You can literally see right into the person's heart and soul. The strongest, most enlightened people no longer conceal or protect themselves from pain, because they are not afraid of suffering. They carry themselves through the world in full view.[21]

When the heart truly listens to another, it is tapping into the inner world of that other person. Asking questions to draw out the other person even further shows true interest in the other person's well-being. This kind of heart is able to enter the world of the other, because in that moment the heart is one with all things. It literally senses no separation. In this state, there is then no other, only one. The "you" and the "I" melt into the oneness of all things. This level of communing with your partner requires the vulnerability of which Dr. Sircus and Brené Brown speak.

It sounds good, doesn't it? But how do you get there?

The path to vulnerability requires humility. You are required to move beyond wanting to look good to an egoless state in which there are no expectations or demands. You simply open up without fear and receive whatever comes. The paradox of vulnerability is that you can only be vulnerable when you are not worried that others will judge you. When you are vulnerable, you become like a turtle without its shell. It takes courage and strength to be your naked, vulnerable self.

Such is the gift of heart vulnerability. With heart vulnerability comes deeper intimacy, connection, and communication with our beloved soulmate. With heart vulnerability we can experience expanded aliveness and love. Before you can open up in a profound way to your partner, you must first practice the art of forgiveness.

The Healing Power of Forgiveness

Forgiveness is a crucial piece of the relationship puzzle. As we have learned through the concept of Wabi Sabi Love, we are imperfect creatures. Forgiveness is integral to our well-being. In fact, forgiveness is what keeps us together when life is tearing us apart.

Forgiveness is not about accepting abuse or bad behavior. It is about freeing yourself from the bad feelings that result from that behavior. Author and speaker Wayne Dyer says: "To forgive is somehow associated with saying that it is all right, that we accept the evil deed. But this is not forgiveness. Forgiveness means that you fill yourself with love and you radiate that love outward and refuse to hang on to the venom or hatred that was engendered by the behaviors that caused the wounds."[22]

Admittedly, some people are easier to love—and forgive—than others. It's easy to love the people who love, support, and nurture you. It's a snap to cherish the ones that show up for you, no matter what. It is infinitely harder to embrace the difficult ones who are judgmental and sometimes downright mean. The people who drive us crazy and spread misery like a contagious disease are the real challenges in our lives. It is difficult to really love those people in the face of their awfulness.

If you have gotten to this point in the book and still think your partner is that person, consider what Marianne Williamson once said: "If you saw a small child fall down and skin their knee, you would quickly wrap your arms around them and give them comfort. But when an adult is acting out and misbehaving or being cruel, we can't see the wounds that are the source of their pain and actions."

Most of the time, whatever the difficult people in our lives are doing or saying has little to do with us. They are merely acting out of old, festering pain. Their disappointment runs deep, and they lash out at the person closest to them, which is you. In that moment of conflict and pain, you become the unfortunate victim of their history.

The challenge for many of us is that we are often related to some of the most difficult people we will ever meet. In those cases, we need to find a way to stay open to loving and accepting them. It all starts with forgiveness. It is not an easy task, especially if your pain and hurt stem from experiences you have shared with them.

In situations in which you find yourself confronted by difficult people, it is time to open up your spiritual toolkit once again. One of my favorite processes harnesses the power of forgiveness. It is also incredibly healing. The process is called Ho'oponopono, an ancient Hawaiian practice of forgiveness and reconciliation.

This tool can be utilized not only for forgiveness, but for all kinds of emotional healing. I first learned about it from Joe Vitale in his book *Zero Limits*. In order to practice Ho'oponopono, you only need one thing: *you*. Begin by taking full responsibility for what is going on. If you feel yourself resisting that thought, take a few deep breaths. Then close your eyes and imagine that you and this difficult person are one single being. Say to yourself, "I love you. Please forgive me. I'm sorry, and thank you."

Ho'oponopono means "to make it right" and is based on the notion that everything you experience is your creation. In other words, anything that is happening—or anything you perceive to be happening—to you in your entire world is made by your hand. Because you create your own reality, you are also 100 percent responsible for that world. You are the mayor of your own town or, to return to an analogy we used earlier in this book, you are the screenwriter, director, and producer of your own movie.

Being responsible does not mean it is your fault. In fact, no fault can be found when we take absolute responsibility. There is no room for it. Because you are responsible for simply everything in the world of your making, you are also tasked with healing yourself. If a person appears in your life as a problem, you are the only one who can change that perception. You do that by simply repeating these four simple phrases several times: "I love you. Please forgive me. I'm sorry, and thank you."

FORGIVENESS HEALING:
THE PROCESS OF HO'OPONOPONO

Bring to mind anyone you need to forgive.

In your mind's eye, construct a small stage below you and place the person there.

Imagine an infinite source of love and healing flowing from a source above the top of your head (from God or your Higher Self). Open up the top of your head and let the source of love and healing flow down inside your body, fill up your body, and overflow out your heart to heal the person on the stage.

Repeat many times: "I love you. Please forgive me. I'm sorry, and thank you."

Next, let go of the person, see him or her floating away, and cut the cord that connects the two of you (if appropriate). If you are forgiving your beloved, then assimilate your beloved inside you.

>
>
> The soul is an infinite ocean of energy and presence made manifest in human form. It's an opportunity to fully express that energy while we are alive. It's an invitation, that we all have, that's wanting to be accepted.
>
> *Panache Desai*

I find that when I practice this exercise, often even daily, my heart opens up and I release the anxiety surrounding the experience. I am literally set free from the pain.

Psychotherapist Fred Luskin, director of the Stanford University Forgiveness Project and author of *Forgive for Good,* has spent more than twenty years studying forgiveness.[23] It starts with identifying exactly how you feel about what happened. Next you promise yourself you will do whatever it takes to make yourself feel better. Then you recognize that forgiveness is not about making up with the other person, but about finding peace within yourself about those past events with that person.

Understand that the continued hurt comes from the feelings you have about the past, not the past itself. Focus your energy on avenues to meet your goals rather than the hurtful experience that disappointed, angered, or crushed you. As my sister, Debbie, once said, the best revenge is your own success. Live your life to the best of your ability instead of spending your time on vengeful thoughts toward the person who harmed you. Change your story of grief to one of forgiveness. Focus on the heroic choice to forgive and move forward in that power forevermore.

According to Luskin, "The practice of forgiveness has been shown to reduce anger, hurt, depression and stress and leads to greater feelings of hope, peace, compassion and self-confidence. Practicing forgiveness leads to healthy relationships as well as physical health. It also influences our attitude, which opens the heart to kindness, beauty, and love."

Small Acts, Big Love

I once heard a quote that still rings true: "If you put each other first, then no one comes in second." Dr. Harry Reis, a psychologist at the University of Rochester, has conducted research showing that people who put their mates' needs first make themselves happier. He calls this "compassionate love." He states: "It's a way of communicating to the other person that you understand what they are all about and that you appreciate and care for them."[24]

This isn't to say that you always put your mate's needs above your own. Obviously you want to be with someone who sometimes does this for you as well. The point is that by consciously caring about your mate's happiness, you will ultimately be happier.

Another way to put it is: "Happy spouse, happy house!"

According to Rabbi Ezagui, marriage is about rising above your own limitations. Marriage is, in his mind, the highest calling of human potential. "Marry yourself first," he advises.

"Marriage begins from within. If I find the soul within me, I can marry someone else and embrace his or her soul. You are not marrying your other half, but marrying yourself."

The Marriage Effect

By now we have dispelled the myths about marriage based on romantic notions with fairy-tale endings. In *The Power of Myth*, Joseph Campbell and Bill Moyers define marriage as something beyond the heady, romantic love we were trained to seek:

> Marriage is not a love affair. A love affair is a totally different thing. A marriage is a commitment to that which you are. That person is literally your other half. And you and the other are one. A love affair isn't that. That is a relationship for pleasure, and when it gets to be unpleasurable, it's off. But a marriage is a life commitment, and a life commitment means the prime concern of your life. If marriage is not the prime concern, you're not married.[25]

Research has proven that happily married couples receive the benefits of something called the "marriage effect," which means that they are:

More likely to live longer

More likely to be physically and mentally healthier and happier

More likely to recover from illness more quickly and
more successfully

A 2007 study found that the rate of death of single men over
age forty was twice as high as that of married men.[26] Marriage
for men is a lifesaver.

Living together is not the same as being married to each
other. It was found that happy couples who are living together
in a committed, unmarried relationship don't receive the
same benefits. I haven't yet found the definitive answer on why
this is true, but when I asked Harville Hendrix about it, he suggested it has something to do with safety and security. On some
unconscious level, those committed but unmarried couples do
not experience the same level of safety that married couples
do. Safety is one of our most profound human needs.

What about those couples who lived together for years very
successfully, but then got married and soon divorced? Harville
says the reason stems from the emergence of the real work of
marriage only after we take those sacred vows. It seems that we
have to work for our security, but the payoff is longevity and a
more stable lifestyle.

We have seen the positive effects marriage can have on our
lives. As we saw in Chapter 6, Wabi Sabi Love is based on the
ability to be honest with yourself and with your partner. It
is the willingness to share your truth, your whole truth, and
nothing but your truth the moment you recognize it.

Recommitting Through New Vows

Perhaps one of you has broken your wedding vows or ignored some or all of what you promised each other. Writing a *relationship vow* affords you the opportunity to describe your renewed commitment to the partnership. Think of it as a mission statement for your relationship that serves as a compass to guide your future actions and stands a testament to your commitment to move toward a shared future. A relationship vow is meant to be a springboard into your new reality, as it informs your beloved of your intention to be greater together than apart.

This exercise allows for a more inspiring future, the very thing that becomes the passionate everyday reality of a couple. Here is one possible relationship vow you can tweak to fit your situation. Fill in the blanks on the right (or download a personal copy of this vow at www.matetosoulmate.com/newvow).

Baby Steps to Long-Lasting Change

At this point, you may still be uncertain about the future of your relationship. Should you stay or should you go? Whichever path you choose, you now have some more tools in your emotional management toolkit to help you through the next phase of your life.

RELATIONSHIP VOW

For the past _____ years we have stood together through sorrow and joy, triumph and defeat, sickness and health, and together we have grown so much. We have evolved and transformed together. We have endured together, laughed, and cried together. *[If applicable:* We have raised a beautiful family together.]

I,_____,

take you, _____,

to be my_____

in cocreating a healthy, loving, supportive relationship as we recommit to a life together as best friends, lovers, and partners. On this day I joyfully promise to wipe away your tears with my laughter and soothe your pain with my caring and compassion. I will be the wind beneath your wings, as we harmonize with a greater understanding of each other. We will heal the misdeeds of the past and renew our life together with honesty and transparency. I give myself to you completely, and I promise to love you always, from this day forth.

I promise to love and cherish you, respect you, and grow with you for all the days of our lives. This is my solemn vow.

I have found that in order for me to make real significant, long-lasting changes, whether it's regarding lifestyle, behavior, or ways of thinking, I need to begin with baby steps. Wherever you are in your relationship right now, none of it happened overnight, and expecting instantaneous change is most likely unreasonable. On some occasions, however, it can happen in an instant, as it did for Stephanie.

Stephanie and her husband, Garth, had been married for many years, but he had always driven her crazy because she is a total "neat freak" and Garth is, well, a bit too comfortable with clutter and overall messiness. When I met Stephanie at a workshop I was leading about Wabi Sabi Love in Sun Valley, Idaho, she explained that Garth's work takes him out of state two weeks of every month and that when he is gone, the house is "her house," and everything is in its place. But when Garth is home the other two weeks, chaos reigns, and no matter how much she begs, nudges, or complains, nothing ever changes.

I had the workshop participants get into groups of three. They were instructed to each share their biggest complaint about their mates and then help each other find a Wabi Sabi Love solution.

Stephanie shared her issue with her teammates, one of whom asked, "Stephanie, do you have a dog?"

"Yes," she said.

"Does your dog shed?"

"Yes."

"What do you do when your dog sheds?"

"I vacuum up the hair."

"Do you still love your dog?"

And then Stephanie got very quiet. She whispered, "Yes, of course," burst out laughing, and said, "Oh my God, Garth sheds!"

And with that realization her world changed. Two words altered her vision of her mate. He sheds. Imagine the freedom in that! Suddenly she saw that just as her dog can't help shedding, neither can Garth. It is just who he is.

Nine months after this happened I called Stephanie to check in with her and see if she was still all right with Garth's "shedding." She said that not only is she still okay with it; their relationship is better than ever because she now spends her time praising him for all the things he does to enhance their connection and life and finds Wabi Sabi solutions for everything else.

As Stephanie's story illustrates, sometimes you can make an instantaneous, life-altering change, but most of us need to commit to taking daily baby steps in order to transform ourselves and our relationship.

A Relationship's Expiration Date

Sometimes great soulmate relationships end. Recognizing that it's time to leave is a heartbreakingly difficult decision.

Movies, media, and our culture in general portray the end of a relationship as a strife-ridden war zone filled with battles over money, kids, property, and even the family pet.

Fortunately, this is slowly beginning to change, thanks in large part to the work of my friend Katherine Woodward Thomas, therapist and relationship expert. Katherine has created a brilliant and innovative process called "conscious uncoupling," a term she coined a few years ago, which has become, overnight, a part of today's lexicon after Gwyneth Paltrow and Chris Martin used it to announce their divorce in 2014.

Through her book *Conscious Uncoupling* and her online workshops, Katherine teaches a five-step process that is designed to leave each individual whole, healthy, and complete rather than wounded, walled off, and significantly broken by the experience.[27] Through conscious uncoupling you release the trauma of the breakup, reclaim your power, and reinvent your life.

Katherine names the three most common reasons people decide to leave:

> The first reason a relationship might end is that one partner has behaved badly and violated the fundamental agreements of the relationship. Perhaps they stole money from the family bank account, had an affair, or are doing drugs or drinking excessively. The second reason is that after years of trying to find ways to peacefully coexist, the residue of built-up resentment, anger, and hurt feelings is unmanageable. The damage done feels too

great to overcome, as little by little the struggles between them have eroded the connection beyond repair for one or both partners. And the third reason is that the couple have simply grown in different directions. It's not uncommon to find couples who once had a shared vision for their lives to find that they are now in very different places with very different values or goals for how they want to spend the rest of their days.

Before calling it quits, Katherine offers three recommendations to those willing to make one final attempt to try to save the partnership:

1. Try couples therapy with a professional counselor to dive deep into all of the issues to see if they can't be resolved in a way that you both can live with.

2. Share your true feelings with your partner without "shaming or blaming," and give your partner a chance to really hear and feel you, so that he or she has the opportunity to rectify the problem.

3. If your partner responds to your concerns by taking concrete actions to improve the situation, do your best to match those efforts with your own and really give it your all before initiating a "conscious uncoupling."

My friend Christine Hohlbaum and her husband of twenty years tried couples therapy only to discover that their irreconcilable differences far outweighed what they still shared. After a painful process that spanned six months, they decided to engage in the conscious uncoupling program to further their understanding of what came next in their lives. Both Christine and her husband did the program separately and at their own pace. It was a deeply spiritual process that caused both of them to grow and to recognize they could bless each other's new path without resentment, anger, or fear.

The day Christine saw her husband's wedding ring on the kitchen shelf, she hugged him and said, "You completed the final session!" With the help of this process, they completely accepted that their soulmate love relationship had morphed into one of friendship. Not only did they benefit from recognizing how their relationship had changed, but their children did as well. They get along better than ever and treat one another with fairness, kindness, and respect. It freed them up to pursue their life's purposes in their own ways: he landed his dream job in a neighboring country and she met her new soulmate who shares so much of what lay dormant inside her for years.

Is He Really My Soulmate?

Although it's true that some soulmate relationships come with an expiration date and aren't meant to last forever, as we discussed in Chapter 8, once you have been in love with someone, your brain is still wired to love that person. If you are open, willing, and available to reignite the love, one place to begin, to turn your mate into your soulmate, is to decide three things:

1. Is he my soulmate?

2. Am I willing to reenvision the way I see him and our relationship?

3. Am I willing to create a new happier, stronger relationship?

If you aren't sure whether he is your soulmate, ponder these questions:

Did I once think of him as my soulmate? If not, what changed?

Now that you have new definitions of what a soulmate is (someone you can completely be yourself with, someone with whom you share unconditional love, and when you look into his eyes you feel at home), ask: Can I now accept him as my soulmate?

Do I love him?

Do I respect him?

Do I find him attractive?

Can I imagine *not* spending the rest of my life with him?

Does spending the rest of my life alone seem more appealing than sticking it out with my mate?

If some of my answers are no, am I willing to entertain the possibility of couples counseling?

Turning Your Mate into Your Soulmate:
16 Steps

Now that you have established a new understanding of love and marriage, you are ready to put the process of turning your mate into your soulmate into practice. Let's begin with a clear intention and then follow along with the gentle "baby" steps that will build your own yellow brick road to a lifetime of love and happiness. You may find it useful to keep a journal while you are taking this journey; in it you can complete the simple exercises and also track your progress. And if you want to be very brave and courageous, share this journal with your partner and encourage him to write in it as well!

Step 1: Create Your Personal Love Intention Statement

A study at Harvard in 1989 showed that those who write down their goals have ten times more success in accomplishing them than those who don't write them down. Another study demonstrated that those who not only wrote down their goals but also shared them with one other person were even more successful. One of the basic principles of manifesting states that "what you put your attention on grows." To have more love in your life, the place to begin is to *be* more of what love is.

Brian has a beautiful love intention that he lives each day: "Everyone I come in contact with will have the experience of being loved."

Mine is: "I am a student of love and a love philanthropist." In addition, I aspire to be more like Brian!

Now write your own love intention statement, a statement that expresses the depth and breadth of your love.

Step 2: Add Pleasure to Your Life

Remember the old saying, "If momma ain't happy, ain't nobody happy!"? It's so very true. Choosing to be responsible for your own happiness can begin right now. Start by figuring out what "happiness" is for you. For me, I find that having a sense of contentment and satisfaction along with knowing and trusting that I live in a friendly Universe is my idea of happiness. I have learned that regardless of circumstances, most of the time I can remember and shift myself into this happy state. My ultimate goal is to reach the state of *santosha*, the Sanskrit word for "imperturbable happiness."

Reducing stress is critical to more happiness. To do so, you need to rebuild the oxytocin levels in your brain. Make sure to plan weekly activities to do that, such as massage, manicures or pedicures, hanging out with girlfriends, having your hair done, and shopping. Also hugs that are twenty seconds or longer are the fastest way to get an oxytocin boost!

Step 3: Define Your Soulmate

Declare that your mate is your soulmate and detail why and how you know this to be true. Once you have done that, buy your beloved a greeting card and include your detailed description in it!

Step 4: Reinvigorate the Story of Your Meeting

Take a trip down memory lane and travel back to the early days of your romance. Write the story of your meeting and recall all the exciting and juicy details of how you came together, including:

Your first positive impression of him

The body part of his you found most attractive

Something funny or kind that you observed him doing

Any feelings you had that he might be "The One"

Positive reactions from family or friends when they first met him

How you felt when he first kissed you

Remember that sharing positive stories about your mate will reinforce sweet feelings, put him in a good light, and create even more love in your relationship. Shifting perspective by emphasizing your mate's positive attributes not only alters the energy within you, but between you too.

Step 5: Create the Space for More Love

Creating the environment for the most amount of love in your relationship may require taking a close look at how you relate to your spouse. Remember that most men desire respect; they want to feel needed and valued the most. Generously praise him for all the things he does right and tell him how and what his actions provide for you.

When speaking to your spouse, remember not to "shame and blame" or be critical. Approach him with kindness in your words, tone of voice, and body language. Make a commitment to do this every day. And when you do need to convey an upset, begin by first telling him five things he has done that you appreciate.

Step 6: Ask for What You Need

Learning to effectively ask for your needs and desires clearly, one request at a time, will make life easier for both of you. Cultivate a culture of impactful communication by learning to listen better too. Review the examples starting on page 47.

Step 7: Learn to Speak the Same Love Language

Imagine what life with your beloved would be like if you each asked the other once a week, "What can I do to make your life better?" It only takes one person to begin making a change, so if you begin this practice today, it's very likely that your partner will reciprocate. Also, if you haven't yet determined your love language and that of your partner, take the quiz at www.5lovelanguages.com. If you can, get your partner to take the quiz at the same time, so you can talk about it together. Once you know his love language, commit to consciously showing your love in the way he will most feel it and hear it.

Step 8: Review Sacred Contracts

Every relationship we have offers us the opportunity to learn and grow. Write down answers to the following questions:

- What are a few of the sacred contracts you and your mate have together?

- What have you learned and continue to learn from each other?

- What were the reasons you came together?

The answers will reveal the sacred contracts you share. Review the contracts in your mind. How can you enhance the terms of the contracts? The answers to these questions will serve as a reminder and a positive incentive to return to the origin of your agreement to be together.

Step 9: Take the Wabi Sabi Amnesty Vow

Imagine how your mate would feel if you promised to never again nag him about that thing he does that bugs you or the thing you most complain about that never changes. In a card or on a piece of notepaper, write the vow on page 248 to your mate (you can also print it out or e-mail it to your partner from www.matetosoulmate.com/amnesty).

Step 10: Wear Rose-Colored Glasses

The couples who consciously choose to wear "rose-colored glasses" have longer, happier, and more satisfying relationships. By wearing rose-colored glasses they are looking for what is right and not for what is wrong. Buy yourself a pair of rose-colored glasses to wear on the days when you find yourself being critical or judgmental.

Step 11: Create Your Shared Vision Statement

Many successful soulmate couples have a shared vision for their partnership. Ours is, "We will make choices and decisions based on what best serves our relationship." By doing this we rarely have to compromise, because when we look at something with a view toward what is best for the partnership, the answer is usually very clear.

Relationship experts Gay and Kathlyn Hendricks, who wrote many bestsellers including *Conscious Loving,* are committed to

WABI SABI AMNESTY VOW

Dear _____ ,

I love you. You are my best friend, lover, and partner.

As you know, for the past ____ years I have been judging you
and nagging you for _____ .

I have recently adopted the concept of Wabi Sabi Love—
learning to find beauty and perfection in imperfection. My gift
and vow to you is to grant you amnesty for this.

With this Wabi Sabi Amnesty Vow, I choose today to release
you from my judgment and to look at this issue differently. My
new story is _____

_____ .

I now vow to do my best to accept you as you are and to
seek and find the beauty and perfection in this habit that has
bothered me in the past.

Please forgive me for all of the times I have blamed, shamed,
judged, or harassed you about this issue.

Thank you for all that you do to make our life wonderful.

Love, _____

P.S. If I begin to slip up (I realize I am not perfect either), I give
you permission to gently put me back on track by simply saying, "Where's the Wabi Sabi Love?"

the following statement: "We expand every day in love and creativity as we inspire others to do the same."

My friends Lisa and Ken have agreed on: "We are best friends who treat each other with love, respect, and kindness."

Take the initiative and write a first draft. Then share it with your partner, so he can add to it until you have a collective vision statement that reflects what you both intend. Once you have your statement, post it someplace where you will both be reminded of it every day, such as the refrigerator door or bathroom mirror. In addition to this, consider recommitting to your relationship through new vows. See the "Relationship Vow" on page 235.

Step 12: Invite God into Your Relationship

Starting a daily practice of gratitude is the easiest way to invite spiritual awareness into your life. Gratitude's healing properties cast away sorrows. In fact, when you are in the space of gratitude, it is impossible to be in fear. It literally shifts your thinking away from what is not possible to what is. Gratitude also makes you more attuned to the Higher Power, which we can access and bring into our relationship at any time.

Step 13: Add in Spice and Adventure

One way to kick-start the romance in your relationship is through the bonding nature and power of an adrenaline rush.

Whether it's a scary movie, bungee jumping, whitewater rafting, or getting on a roller coaster, plan an adventure with your honey and try something new and adventurous.

Step 14: Practice Forgiveness of Yourself and Your Partner

Forgiveness is a gift we give ourselves, so that we may have peace of mind. It doesn't mean we forget or allow toxic people or situations to remain in our lives. It is not a process of reconciliation, but rather being willing to let go of hurt, anger, and resentments. Fred Luskin teaches that forgiving leads to greater feelings of hope, peace, compassion, and self-confidence. "If you've been treated badly, and you don't really heal, you're going to be less trusting, more defensive, and more quarrelsome," says Luskin.

Pastor and author Rick Warren says resentment is "a self-inflicted wound. Whenever you're resentful, it always hurts you more than the person you're bitter against. In fact, while you're still worrying about something that happened years ago, they've forgotten about it! Your past is past, and it can't hurt you any more unless you hold on to it."[28]

A study at Duke University showed that forgiving and letting go of old grudges reduces levels of depression, anxiety, and anger. People who forgive tend to have better relationships, feel happier and more optimistic overall, and enjoy better psychological well-being. One way to begin would be to practice the forgiveness process of Ho'oponopono found on page 229.

Step 15: Open Up to Vulnerability

If you were to peek inside the human brain, I bet you'd find the emotions of fear and vulnerability side by side. It is scary to open yourself up in new ways, because you have no experience of knowing what will happen if you do. So many of us shut ourselves down as an act of self-protection in the belief that the bad we do know is most likely better than the good we might come to know if we become vulnerable. Vulnerability, however, is the only way to intimacy. And intimacy is the glue in a long-lasting relationship.

Practice sharing just one small thing with your partner that you might not have shared for fear of the reaction you might get. It can be as simple as sharing your opinion about something in the news or the movie you just saw together. The only way to get to something new is to behave in a new way. Your mate just might surprise you by acting differently too.

Step 16: Do the Intimacy Exercise to Deepen and Reconnect

Find ninety minutes to spend alone with your partner and take turns asking each other the thirty-six deep and probing questions of the Intimacy Exercise found starting on page 211. After you have answered all the questions, stand or sit across from each other and lightly gaze into each other's eyes for four minutes in silence.

Take your time with this program of renewal. You may experience setbacks, which are normal whenever you try something new. Changing habits doesn't happen overnight, but sometimes epiphanies do. These steps will accelerate the process of turning your mate into your soulmate. Follow them and watch what happens next!

Flawed and Fabulous

Congratulations. You have gotten this far. If you haven't noticed by now, messy, sweaty, crazy love is what life is all about. The road is never perfect. Nothing ever is. We human beings may be flawed, but that doesn't mean we can't have fabulous relationships.

Author and energy healer Courtney A. Walsh writes about love, life, and all things wonderful. One of her most famous letters is called "Dear Human":

Dear Human:

You've got it all wrong. You didn't come here to master unconditional love. That is where you came from and where you'll return. You came here to learn personal love.

Universal love. Messy love. Sweaty love. Crazy love. Broken love. Whole love.

Infused with divinity. Lived through the grace of stumbling. Demonstrated through the beauty of . . . messing up. Often.

You didn't come here to be perfect. You already are. You came here to be gorgeously human. Flawed and fabulous.

And then to rise again into remembering.

But unconditional love? Stop telling that story. Love, in truth, doesn't need ANY other adjectives. It doesn't require modifiers. It doesn't require the condition of perfection. It only asks that you show up. And do your best. That you stay present and feel fully.

That you shine and fly and laugh and cry and hurt and heal and fall and get back up and play and work and live and die as YOU.

It's enough. It's Plenty.[29]

Breathe in the power of Courtney's words. Print out her missive as a reminder when you forget that it really is okay to be flawed and fabulous. Post it on your desk, your bathroom mirror, or your bedroom door. Remember that love needs no adjectives. Love is love. It is where we came from. It is the place to which we will all return.

The point is to live love now, the very best you can.

Creating Your Lifetime of Love

The most important conversation in the world is the one we have in our own heads every day. And, unfortunately, according to scientists, we have about sixty thousand thoughts a day. That means that every day most people have more than forty-five thousand negative thoughts. It's been proven that "our beliefs become our biology." Every little thing about our lives is directly affected by our thoughts. Thus, our internal dialogue impacts every area of our life from our health to our finances to our love life.

In a *Redbook* article, Hannah Hickok quotes psychologist Vagdevi Meunier, founder of the Center for Relationships: "If you're engaging in hopeless, negative, or judgmental self-talk [about your spouse], you're actually having a stronger relationship with the spouse inside your head than the real person." Hickok herself continues, "Shifting to more positive, vulnerable, empathetic self-talk—with the partner in your head *and* in your life—can help reframe your dynamic. In other words, instead of wondering, *Do I still love him?* think, *I love him because I choose to see all the things that make him wonderful.*"[30]

This requires that we put on our big-girl pants and be willing to be emotionally mature adults. It is about managing our thoughts, beliefs, and emotions. By letting our "monkey mind" run continual negative conversations in our head about our mate, we create a poisonous, unwinnable situation.

Assuming that your relationship isn't burdened by abuse, addiction, or intolerable bad behavior (all of which require professional couples counseling), it's really up to you to decide to become a "student of love" and take the baby steps necessary to reenvision and reignite your love and passion. You now have a myriad of ways to positively impact the future of your relationship. The really great news is that it takes only you—

one person—to get the ball rolling in the right direction. Once you begin the process, most likely your partner will respond in ways that will delight and surprise you.

Real change is possible, and you can make it a fun and enjoyable process. Think of it this way. Imagine that for the past five, ten, or twenty years (maybe more) you have had a large fish tank in your living room. When you first set it up, everything was new and beautiful. You filled your fish tank with freshwater and colorful fish, and for a while you remembered to empty the tank and clean it on a regular basis. Your fish tank was the focal point of your home. Every evening, with a glass of wine in hand, you and your honey would sit on the couch and enjoy the sensual movements of the fish swimming to and fro while you listened to the soft gurgling sounds of the pump. Over the years you got busy with work, the kids, and life in general, and eventually the water in the tank got cloudy. Mold began to grow on the glass and the fish began to die off. When you took a moment to really look at the tank, you wondered whether you should finally get rid of it or take the time to bring it back to life.

If you have read this far, chances are you are seriously ready to refurbish your tank. You are now prepared to consider bringing your relationship back to life. If you are not yet 100 percent committed to improving your relationship, consider this: more than 50 percent of first marriages (in the U.S.), 67 percent of second, and 73 percent of third marriages end in divorce. Why? Quite often because we haven't learned the lessons of the past and make the same mistakes over and over again, creating similar conflicts.

Although I haven't yet invented the magic wand to turn your mate into your soulmate, it can happen in a Wabi Sabi Love transformational instant. Think back to the story about Stephanie and Garth. Once Stephanie realized that "Garth sheds," her relationship changed from mediocre to great. In the story about Inga and Jack Canfield, when Inga decided to be Jack's "refueling station," she radically transformed her commitment to their relationship. By doing this, Inga not only created a new container for their love and marriage; she also practiced what my beloved Brian calls "soulmate math." In basic arithmetic, one plus one equals two. In soulmate math, one plus one equals eleven and your love blesses the world.

Turning our mate into our soulmate is a process that requires daily attention, if not the occasional minute-by-minute effort when we must remember to *choose love*. Choosing love is when we realize that our partner's happiness is as important to us as our own happiness and that we are committed to sharing with that person our appreciation, affection, and attention.

One way to *choose love* is to practice generosity and kindness. A study examining the role of generosity in marriage, by the University of Virginia's National Marriage Project, found that the virtue of giving good things to one's spouse freely and abundantly is a way that couples can build a strong, stable partnership.[31] The questions in the study were directed in three areas. Did spouses offer small kindnesses to each other? Did they regularly express affection? Were they able to forgive? It's clear that small daily doses of kindness and generosity can have a big impact on the happiness level in your relationship.

One thing I know with 98 percent certainty is this: your partner didn't wake up this morning thinking, "How can I make my spouse crazy today?!" Just like you and me, our partners want to be loved and accepted for who they are—warts and all. When we can learn to shift our perception of them and embrace them for the flawed yet lovable human beings that they are, everyone wins at love, and the prize for both of you is a love bigger and more delicious than anything you ever imagined.

A lifetime of soulmate love is a delicious soup of chemistry, communication, compatibility, connection, vulnerability, and the choices we make to wear our rose-colored glasses. We all want and need a partner who will be our lover, best friend, ally, and soft place to land. We want someone with whom we can completely be ourselves, someone who will love us on our good days and—most important—on our bad days too. When we find ourselves noticing or even obsessing about our partner's imperfections, we remember to stop and manage our thoughts and reframe them in a positive manner.

And if you are really stuck in negativity, ponder my favorite line from *A Course in Miracles:* "The only thing that can be lacking in any situation is that which you are not giving." Ask yourself, if maybe, just maybe, you are willing, in that moment, to let go of any judgments you are having and allow yourself to be more accepting, loving, kind, and compassionate.

Throughout these pages the essential truths about what happy couples do to keep the fires of love burning strong have been illuminated. The lessons are simple, yet the results can be life-changing.

- Express your love and affection—often.

- Show care. It's the little gestures that mean everything.

- Learn to love what your partner loves, so you can participate in some of his or her passions.

- Practice vulnerability and share yourself with authenticity and honesty, always with tremendous love, kindness, and generosity.

- Remember to find the beauty and perfection in the imperfection.

The choice is yours. You now know what a true soulmate is, and although yours didn't arrive with a personal "owner's manual," my dream is that this book can serve as a guide and a reminder for you on how to navigate this journey of love—together.

Acknowledgments

The idea for this book first blossomed in a conversation with my amazing friend Lisa Sharkey. *The Soulmate Secret* had just been released. She congratulated me and then said, "It's wonderful that you've written a book for single people, but next time tell me how to turn my mate into my soulmate." That idea floated around in my mind for years, and the result is the book you now hold in your hands.

There are literally dozens of people whose love and support I am so grateful for. My sister, the fabulous Debbie Ford: your whisperings and direction from the "other side" came through loud and clear. Christine Hohlbaum, my friend and editor, who worked side by side with me (even though she was in Germany): I couldn't have done this without you; your creative skills, commitment, and sparkling energy are evident on every page. Nick Ortner: a big thanks to you for compassionately "tapping" me through my initial resistance to writing this book.

I am exceedingly grateful to the fearless souls who shared their wisdom, research, and stories with me, including Carol Allen, Alison Armstrong, Dr. Arthur Aron, Heide Banks, Gabrielle Bernstein, Mat Boggs, Brené Brown, Inga and Jack Canfield, Carlos Cavallo, Gary Chapman, Diane V. Cirincione and Jerry Jampolsky, Otto and Susie Collins, Panache Desai, Hale Dwoskin, Donna Eden and David Feinstein, Rabbi Baruch Ezagui, Dr. Helen Fisher, Elizabeth Gilbert, Vivian Glyck, Dr. John Gottman, John Gray, Gay and Kathlyn Hendricks, Harville Hendrix and Helen LaKelly Hunt, Reverend Cynthia James, Matt Licata, Lana Love and David Almeida, Fred Luskin, Jill Mangino and Ray Dunn, Peggy McColl and Denis Beliveau, Pujya Swamiji, Stephanie Reed, Lynn Rose and Bob Doyle, Sadhvi Bhagawati Saraswati, Linda Sivertsen, Katherine Woodward Thomas, Joe Vitale, Neale Donald Walsch, Courtney A. Walsh, and Marianne Williamson.

To my dream team at HarperElixir, Claudia Boutote, Gideon Weil, Mark Tauber, Melinda Mullin, Laina Adler, Jenn Jensen, Suzanne Quist, Terri Leonard, Hilary Lawson, and Adrian Morgan: thank you for your love, creativity, and support for this book.

To my PR angel, Jill Mangino: thank you for always caring and for looking for ways to keep spreading the word. To Rita Curtis: I am indebted to you for launching and sustaining my speaking career. You are a gem and a good friend.

To my family at Evolving Wisdom, Claire Zammit, Craig Hamilton, and the entire team: thank you for the difference you are making in the world and for inviting me into the circle; I feel honored to be a part of such a talented and dedicated group of evolutionary souls.

To Doc Childre, Deborah Rozman, Howard Martin, and the entire team at HeartMath Institute: much gratitude goes to you for your pioneering and groundbreaking contributions in the domain of heart intelligence; you have changed and positively impacted my life in ways big and small.

To my mother, Sheila Fuerst: endless blessings for the loving and bright light you always shine on us.

Finally, to my soulmate and beloved husband, Brian Hilliard, who supported me through this process from beginning to end: there are no words to describe my deep love and appreciation for the ongoing love and care I receive from you moment by moment; thank you for loving me the way that you do; thank you for always being my safe place to land; I love you.

Resources

CAROL ALLEN is a happily married Vedic astrologer, relationship coach, and the author of *Love Is in the Stars: The Wise Woman's Astrological Guide to Men*. Carol has been featured on E!, *Bridezillas, Extra,* and *Dr. Drew's Lifechangers*. Whether you want to deepen a relationship or heal lifelong love patterns, shape your romantic destiny with Carol's free newsletter, catalog of books, personalized astrology reports, and programs. *www.loveisinthestars.com*

ALISON ARMSTRONG explores the good reasons behind the behavior of men and women, such as fundamental differences in the ways we think, act, and communicate. She offers simple, partnership-based solutions to improve our communication and intimacy by honoring ourselves and others. She's known for her insight, sense of humor, and ability to articulate the human experience and predicament of gender. *www.understandmen.com*

HEIDE BANKS helps individuals free themselves of past hurts and relationships, so that they can move forward in their lives and experience greater loving, joy, and fulfillment. There are many invisible things that hinder our ability to achieve success in our relationships. Heide works energetically, and psychologically, drawing on over twenty years experience as a relationship coach to identify these patterns and help people release them, so that they are free to experience the love they are meant to have.

www.heidebanks.com

GABRIELLE BERNSTEIN has been named "a new thought leader" by Oprah Winfrey. She appears regularly as an expert on *The Dr. Oz Show* and was named "a new role model" by the *New York Times*. Gabrielle is the *New York Times* bestselling author of the books *May Cause Miracles* and *Miracles Now*. Her other titles include *Add More ~ing to Your Life* and *Spirit Junkie*. Gabrielle, a "spiritual activist," recently teamed up with Deepak Chopra to cohost the *Guinness Book of World Records* largest group meditation. For more on Gabrielle's work, visit *www. gabbyb.tv,* or join her social networking community enabling women to empower, inspire, and connect at *www.herfuture.com*.

MAT BOGGS is the bestselling coauthor of *Project Everlasting* and creator of Cracking the Man Code. He has appeared on *The*

Today Show, CNN's *Headline News, Showbiz Tonight,* the Style Network, and many more. As a highly acclaimed speaker and love coach, Mat specializes in helping women "manifest their man" and attract the relationship they desire.
www.crackingthemancode.com

OTTO AND SUSIE COLLINS are married soulmates, authors, speakers, and coaches committed to helping people all over the world bring more love, intimacy, passion, and connection into their relationships and lives. Their love and relationship book and audio titles include *Red Hot After 50, Hypnotize His Heart,* and *Magic Relationship Words.* To learn more about Susie and Otto and tap into their relationship and life wisdom, visit *www.susieandotto.com.*

PANACHE DESAI is a contemporary thought leader whose gift of vibrational transformation has drawn thousands of people from around the world. Not aligned with any religious or spiritual tradition, he acts as a direct line to divine consciousness, empowering people to free themselves of pain, suffering, sadness, and self-limiting beliefs.
www.panachedesai.com

HALE DWOSKIN is the *New York Times* bestselling author of *The Sedona Method* and is featured in the movie *Letting Go.*

He is the CEO and director of training of Sedona Training Associates, an organization that teaches courses based on the emotional releasing techniques inspired by his mentor, Lester Levenson. Hale is an international speaker and featured faculty member at Esalen and the Omega Institute. He is also one of the twenty-four featured teachers of the book and movie phenomenon *The Secret* as well as a founding member of the Transformational Leadership Council. For over three decades, he has regularly been teaching the Sedona Method to individuals and corporations throughout the United States and the United Kingdom and has been leading coach trainings and advanced retreats since the early 1990s. He is also the coauthor, with Lester Levenson, of *Happiness Is Free: And It's Easier Than You Think!* (a five-book series).

www.sedona.com

During their thirty-nine years together, DONNA EDEN and DAVID FEINSTEIN have built the world's largest and most vibrant organization teaching Energy Medicine. Their more than 1,100 certified practitioners are serving thousands of clients and teaching hundreds of classes in the United States, Canada, Latin America, Europe, Asia, and Australia. Together they have written four award-winning books, including their most recent on their favorite topic, *The Energies of Love*. Donna is among the most sought-after, most joyous, and most authoritative spokespersons for Energy Medicine, and her healing abilities are legendary. Learn more at *www.learnenergy medicine.com*. David, a clinical psychologist, is a pioneer and leader in Energy Psychology. Learn more at *www.energy psyched.com*.

RABBI BARUCH EZAGUI is director of the Chabad organization in La Jolla, California. Chabad, a Hebrew acronym for "wisdom, understanding, and knowledge," is an intellectual-mystical Jewish movement begun 250 years ago as a branch of Hasidism. Its global vision is to inspire all of humanity to find its highest common denominator and uncover heaven here on earth. With approximately five thousand centers worldwide, it seeks to respond to religious, social, and humanitarian needs around the world. Rabbi Ezagui is committed to assisting individuals from any background in reaching their potential. *www.chabadoflajolla.com*

HELEN FISHER, PH.D., professor at Rutgers University, is an anthropologist and one of the world's leading experts and researchers on love and brain chemistry.
www.theanatomyoflove.com

VIVIAN GLYCK is the founder of Just Like My Child Foundation and the creator of the Girl Power Project, an educational program focused on keeping one million vulnerable girls safe from rape, disease, early pregnancy, and dropping out of school. *www.justlikemychild.org*

JOHN GOTTMAN and his wife, Julie, are cofounders of the Gottman Institute, an internationally renowned organization dedicated to combining wisdom from over four decades of research and practice to support and strengthen marriages and relationships by offering workshops and resources for couples, families, and professionals. The Gottman Method uses a practical approach to help couples break through barriers to achieve greater understanding, connection, and intimacy in their relationships. *www.gottman.com*

JOHN GRAY, relationship counselor, lecturer, and author, has written seventeen books on relationships and personal growth, including one of the all-time bestsellers, *Men Are from Mars, Women Are from Venus.* On his website, you will learn new skills for improving communication and getting what you want in your relationships, inside and outside of the bedroom. Beyond relationship skills, you will also learn to add the important nutrients to your diet to boost your energy, enjoy better sleep, balance your hormones, increase your libido, and stabilize positive moods. This nutritional aspect is essential to experience a lifetime of love and passion. *www.marsvenus.com*

HEARTMATH is a world leader in the areas of heart-rate variability (HRV), stress, and wellness. HeartMath and its sister company, the nonprofit HeartMath Institute, have spent over two decades researching and educating professionals and consumers about HRV feedback and HRV coherence training and their role in stress relief, emotional self-regulation, and increased performance and wellness. They've developed research-based tools and technologies that empower people to self-regulate emotions and improve quality of life.
www.heartmath.com

GAY AND KATHLYN HENDRICKS offer live and virtual seminars on the core skills of conscious loving and conscious living. A key distinguishing feature of their work is a focus on body intelligence, using the organic skills of breathing, movement, and authentic communication to create a felt experience of well-being and intimacy.
www.hendricks.com

HARVILLE HENDRIX, PH.D., AND HELEN LAKELLY HUNT, PH.D., cocreated Imago Relationship Theory and Therapy, practiced by over twelve hundred Imago therapists in thirty-seven countries, and have produced ten books, including three *New York Times* bestsellers. This husband and wife team of thirty-two years recently founded a nonprofit that offers free relationship education through Safe Conversations workshops, which seek to interrupt the downward cycle of

poverty, ensure greater health and economic security for families, reduce violence, and strengthen communities.
www.harvilleandhelen.com
www.familywellnessdallas.org/#home

CHRISTINE HOHLBAUM is an engaging public speaker on time-management practices, blogging, and a range of lifestyle issues. At TEDxLinz in Austria she spoke about the Slow movement based on her most recent release, *The Power of Slow: 101 Ways to Save Time in Our 24/7 World.* She works as a writer and PR consultant in Freiburg, Germany.
www.powerofslow.com

CYNTHIA JAMES is a transformational speaker, teacher, and coach whose work helps people move from being overworked and overwhelmed to enjoying lasting health in mind, body, and spirit. Her emotional integrative techniques assist people in activating the power of choice. Shifting of thought patterns and behaviors creates balance personally and professionally. Clients consistently walk away feeling more self-aware, confident, and clear. They are awakened to the inherent power within them and how they can make a difference in the world.
www.cynthiajames.net

JERRY JAMPOLSKY, M.D., AND DIANE CIRINCIONE-JAMPOLSKY, PH.D., bestselling authors, share their his-

toric work of Attitudinal Healing through their books, CDs, DVDs, podcasts, articles, and events.
www.ahinternational.org

MATT LICATA, PH.D., is a psychotherapist in private practice in Boulder, Colorado, where he works in person and via Skype with patients and clients around the world. He is editor of *A Healing Space* blog and has worked in the publishing field for over twenty years.
www.mattlicataphd.com

LANA LOVE AND DAVID ALMEIDA host an Internet talk radio show entitled *Universal Soul Love.* They say: "Universal Soul Love is a humanitarian project committed to raising the conscious vibration of humanity. Universal Love is not just the expression of unconditional love by an individual. It is the group experience of higher love shared by many people. Universal love is kindness, compassion, and empathy for all living beings. This high vibration allows for the greatest expansion of consciousness, and supports the divine plan of the universe."
www.universalsoullove.com
www.bbsradio.com/universalsoullove

FRED LUSKIN is one of the world's leading researchers and teachers on the subject of forgiveness. Author of the bestseller *Forgive for Good: A Proven Prescription for Health and Happiness,* he is a professor of clinical psychology at the Institute of

Transpersonal Psychology and has directed the Stanford Forgiveness Project for twenty years.
www.learningtoforgive.com

JILL MANGINO is the president of Circle 3 Media, a boutique public-relations and conscious media consulting agency. She lives with her fiancé, Ray, and their six furry babies in rural New Jersey.
www.circle3media.com

PEGGY MCCOLL is a *New York Times* bestselling author who has written ten books. She is recognized as the go-to expert in helping authors write their books, turn them into bestsellers, and make money doing what they love. She is known as the "Bestseller Maker."
www.peggymccoll.com

NICK ORTNER is a *New York Times* bestselling author and the creator and executive producer of the hit documentary film *The Tapping Solution.* He has also produced the Tapping World Summit, an annual worldwide online event that has been attended by over a hundred thousand people. Ortner is a dynamic speaker, presenting breakthrough live tapping sessions around the world. He lives in Newtown, Connecticut, with his wife, Brenna, and their daughter.
www.thetappingsolution.com

LYNN ROSE is an expert in "WOW Performance" in life, business, and events. Seen on CBS, NBC, FOX, among others, as an entertainer and TV host, Lynn has opened for celebrities around the world. As CEO of two six-figure businesses, she's known as the "secret sauce" for industry leaders because of her media and marketing expertise. She brings energizing entertainment, emceeing, and empowering training for hundreds of thousands around the world. Clients include Fortune 500 corporations, entrepreneurial organizations, and events. *www.lynnrose.com*

SADHVI BHAGAWATI SARASWATI, PH.D., is president of the Divine Shakti Foundation, bringing education and empowerment to women and children; secretary-general of Global Interfaith WASH Alliance; and director of the International Yoga Festival. Sadhviji graduated from Stanford University and has lived at Parmarth Niketan, Rishikesh, India, for nearly twenty years with her guru, Pujya Swami Chidanand Saraswatiji, where she gives spiritual discourses, counseling, and coaching and oversees a myriad of charitable programs. *www.sadhviji.org*

MARK SIRCUS, AC., O.M.D., D.M.(P.), is an acupuncturist and a doctor of oriental and pastoral medicine. For many years Dr. Sircus has been researching the human condition and the causes of disease; he has distilled many of the diverse medical systems into a new form of medicine that he calls Natural Allopathic Medicine.

www.drsircus.com

KATHERINE WOODWARD THOMAS, M.A., M.F.T., is the author of the national bestsellers *Calling in "The One": 7 Weeks to Attract the Love of Your Life* and *Conscious Uncoupling: 5 Steps to Living Happily Even After.* Her in-person and virtual seminars have helped tens of thousands of people find and keep soulmate love or, as is sometimes appropriate, end their romantic relationships with love and honor.

www.katherinewoodwardthomas.com

JOE VITALE is the author of many bestselling books including *The Attractor Factor, Life's Missing Instruction Manual, The Key, Faith, Attract Money Now,* and *At Zero,* the sequel to his bestseller *Zero Limits.* He created the Miracles Coaching program and helps people achieve their dreams by understanding the deeper aspects of the Law of Attraction and the Law of Right Action. This man was once homeless, but today is a bestselling author who believes in magic and miracles.

www.joevitale.com

NEALE DONALD WALSCH has written extensively about relationships and the role of the soul in our lives in his Conversations with God series. Several additional books explain and extend their message. He regularly explores these matters further and discusses them personally with anyone who wishes to do so at *www.cwgconnect.com*.

COURTNEY A. WALSH is an author, speaker, blogger, channel, medium, energy healer, and social media figure. Her manifesto for love, entitled "Dear Human," went viral and was shared by over ten million people worldwide. She speaks on suicide prevention, wholeness-based wellness, bullying awareness, and empowerment for all.
www.squeezingthestars.com

MARIANNE WILLIAMSON is an internationally acclaimed spiritual author and lecturer. Six of her eleven books have been *New York Times* bestsellers; four have been number one *New York Times* bestsellers. *A Return to Love* is considered a must read in the area of the New Spirituality. The paragraph from that book beginning "Our deepest fear is not that we are inadequate. Our deepest fear is that we are powerful beyond measure" is considered an anthem for the contemporary generation of seekers.
www.marianne.com

Notes

1. Bob Grant, "Male and Female Brains Wired Differently," *The Scientist*, December 4, 2013, http://www.the-scientist.com/?articles.view/articleNo/38539/title/Male-and-Female-Brains-Wired-Differently/.

2. J. K. Rempel, J. G. Holmes, and M. P. Zanna, "Trust in Close Relationships," *Journal of Personality and Social Psychology* 49(1) (July 1985): 95–112.

3. Brené Brown, "Listening to Shame," *Ted Talk*, March 2012, https://www.ted.com/talks/brene_brown_listening_to_shame.

4. Download a free eBook version of the book, which has been retitled *The Everything Book: The Essential Details About the One You Love*, at www.soulmatesecret.com/everything.

5. K. T. Buehlman, J. M. Gottman, and L. F. Katz, "How a Couple Views Their Past Predicts Their Future," *Journal of Family Psychology* 5(3–4) (March/June 1992): 295–318.

6. Yanki Tauber, "What Is a Soul?" http://www.chabad.org/library/article_cdo/aid/3194/jewish/What-is-a-Soul.htm.

7. The following is based on the personal story of Donna Eden and David Feinstein as told in their book, *The Energies of Love: Using Energy Medicine to Keep Your Relationship Thriving* (New York: Tarcher/Penguin, 2014).

8. http://bbsradio.com/universalsoullove.

9. Emily Esfahani Smith, "Science Says Lasting Relationships Come Down to Two Basic Traits," *The Atlantic,* November 9, 2014, http://www.businessinsider.com/lasting-relationships-rely-on-2-traits-2014-11.

10. Sandra Murray, et al., "Tempting Fate or Inviting Happiness? Unrealistic Idealization Prevents the Decline of Marital Satisfaction," *Psychological Science,* April 2011, doi: 10.1177/0956797611403155.

11. Mark Banschick, "The High Failure Rate of Second and Third Marriages," *Psychology Today,* February 6, 2012, https://www.psychology-today.com/blog/the-intelligent-divorce/201202/the-high-failure-rate-second-and-third-marriages.

12. Interview with Marianne Williamson in the Art of Love Relationship Series, 2013.

13. Marianne Williamson, *Illuminata: A Return to Prayer* (New York: Riverhead, 1994), pp.158–60.

14. Foundation for Inner Peace, *A Course in Miracles* (Mill Valley, CA: Foundation for Inner Peace, 1992), p. 28.

15. Leil Lowndes, "How Neuroscience Can Help Us Find True Love," *The Wall Street Journal (Speakeasy),* February 14, 2013, http://blogs.wsj.com/speakeasy/2013/02/14/how-neuroscience-can-help-us-find-true-love/.

16. D. G. Dutton and A. P. Aron, "Some Evidence for Heightened Sexual Attraction Under Conditions of High Anxiety," *Journal of Personality and Social Psychology* 30(4) (October 1974): 510–17.

17. Arthur Aron, et al., "The Experimental Generation of Interpersonal Closeness: A Procedure and Some Preliminary Findings," *Personality and Social Psychology Bulletin* 23(4) (April 1997): 363–77.

18. Mandy Len Catron, "To Fall in Love with Anyone, Do This," *New York Times,* January 9, 2015, http://mobile.nytimes.com/2015/01/11/fashion/modern-love-to-fall-in-love-with-anyone-do-this.html?referrer&_r=1.

19. Carissa Ray, "Can 36 Questions Help You Fall Back in Love? Putting Our Marriage to the Test," *Today,* January 22, 2015, http://www.today.com/health/can-36-questions-help-you-fall-back-love-putting-our-2D80438436.

20. Brené Brown, "The Price of Invulnerability," *TedxTalks,* October 12, 2010, http://tedxtalks.ted.com/video/TEDxKC-Bren-Brown-The-Price-of;search%3Atag%3A%22TEDxKC%22.

21. Mark Sircus, "The Heart Is the Vulnerability of Being," June 20, 2012, http://www.drsircus.com/spiritual-psychology/heart-vulnerability.

22. Wayne Dyer, "Forgiveness," *Living Life Fully,* http://www.livinglife fully.com/flo/flobeforgiveness.htm.

23. Fred Luskin, "Forgive for Good," http://learningtoforgive.com/9-steps.

24. Quoted in Elizabeth Bernstein, "Small Acts, Big Love: People Who Put Their Mates' Needs First Make Themselves Happier Too," *The Wall Street Journal,* February 12, 2013, http://www.wsj.com/articles/SB100 01424127887323696404578297942503592524.

25. Joseph Campbell and Bill Moyers, *The Power of Myth* (New York: Anchor, 1991), p. 250.

26. Health.com, "Is Love Better for Men's or Women's Health?" June 3, 2012, *Fox News Magazine,* http://magazine.foxnews.com/food-wellness/love-better-mens-or-womens-health.

27. Katherine Woodward Thomas, *Conscious Uncoupling: A 5-Week Program to Release the Trauma of a Breakup, Reclaim Your Power & Reinvent Your Life,* http://evolvingwisdom.com/consciousuncoupling /digital-course/.

28. Rick Warren, "Why Should You Forgive?" May 21, 2014, http://rick warren.org/devotional/english/why-should-you-forgive.

29. Courtney Walsh, "Dear Human," *Soul-Lit: A Journal of Spiritual Poetry,* http://soul-lit.com/poems/v4/Walsh/index.html; see also http:// www.courtneyawalsh.com.

30. Hannah Hickok, "How to Fall Back in Love with Your Husband," *Redbook,* October 28, 2014, http://www.redbookmag.com/love-sex /relationships/a19288/fall-back-in-love/.

31. Tara Parker-Pope, "The Generous Marriage," *New York Times,* December 8, 2011, http://well.blogs.nytimes.com/2011/12/08/is-generosity-better-than-sex/?_r=0.

Credits

pp. 104–5: Definition of the soul by Yanki Tauber, from "What Is a Soul?" (www.chabad.org/library/article_cdo/aid/3194/jewish/What -is-a-Soul.htm). Reprinted by permission of Chabad.org.

pp. 110–15: The personal story of Donna Eden and David Feinstein as told in their book *The Energies of Love: Using Energy Medicine to Keep Your Relationship Thriving*. Copyright © 2014 by Donna Eden and David Feinstein. Published by Tarcher/Penguin. Used with permission of Donna Eden and David Feinstein.

p. 145: Chart of tapping points, from www.TheTappingSolution.com. Reprinted by permission of Nick Ortner.

pp. 144–50: Tapping technique statements, from Nick Ortner, as used in his workshops. Reprinted by permission of Nick Ortner.

pp. 182–83: "Prayers for Couples," pp. 158–60 in *Illuminata: A Return to Prayer*, by Marianne Williamson. Copyright © 1994 by Marianne Williamson. Published by Riverhead Books. Reprinted by permission of Marianne Williamson.

pp. 211–14: The thirty-six questions of the Intimacy Exercise, pp. 374–75 in Arthur Aron, et al., "The Experimental Generation of Interpersonal Closeness: A Procedure and Some Preliminary Findings," *Personality and Social Psychology Bulletin* 23(4) (April 1997): 363–77. Reprinted by permission of SAGE publications.

pp. 252–53: "Dear Human," by Courtney A. Walsh. First posted on Facebook, August 12, 2012, by Courtney A. Walsh. Reprinted by permission of Courtney A. Walsh.

About the Author

Arielle Ford is a leading personality in the personal growth and contemporary spirituality movement. For the past twenty-five years she has been living, teaching, and promoting consciousness through all forms of media. She is a relationship expert, speaker, blogger for *The Huffington Post,* and the producer and host of Evolving Wisdom's Art of Love Relationship series.

Arielle is a gifted writer and the author of ten books including the international bestseller *The Soulmate Secret: Manifest the Love of Your Life with the Law of Attraction.* She has been called "The Cupid of Consciousness" and "The Fairy Godmother of Love."

She lives in La Jolla, California, with her husband and soulmate, Brian Hilliard, and their feline friends. Visit her at www .arielleford.com.

Also by

Arielle Ford

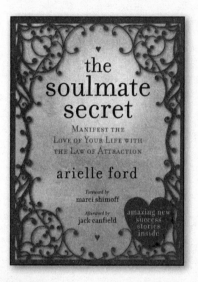

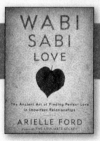

**Available wherever books
and e-books are sold**

HARPER**ELIXIR**